Three Polish-American Catholic Parishes

Research by Jean Marie Miscisin, MLS, MA

DEDICATION

This research is dedicated to ALL FAITHFUL CATHOLICS and all sincere seekers of the TRUTH.

This manuscript, Three Polish-American Catholic Parishes, reports the interpretation and application of one section of the documents of the Second Vatican Council that opened on October 11, 1962.

In this manuscript, Three Polish-American Catholic Parishes, different degrees of assimilation and ethnic pluralism for each parish are reported from a sociological perspective. Conclusions were drawn by comparing the roles of the parishes historically, demographically, and following with trilateral correspondence analysis.

Three Polish-American Catholic Parishes

CONTENTS

1. Statement of Purpose & Perspective

The Triple Melting Pot

The Unmeltable Ethnics

Methodology

At least three views of American culture are expressed today. The first two conceptions require major changes in the immigrant's way of life:

1. Assimilation is "Anglo-Conformity" in which the immigrant is expected to adopt English institutions (as modified by the American Revolution), the English language, and English oriented cultural patterns as dominant and standard in American life. (Gordon in Meister, 1974:86)

"Americanization" is a high-powered form of assimilation, a planned program to delineate all "Cultural Baggage," and remake the immigrant into an "American"; stripping him of native culture and attachments including mode of dress, customs, values, and most of all language. (Gordon in Meister, 1974:86)

2. The "melting pot" perspective wherein all citizens contribute to and absorb each other's cultural values and customs has the end result of a whole new entity, "the American." (Gordon in Meister, 1974:88)

3. In "Cultural Pluralism" each ethnic and/or racial group preserves its own language, religion, communal institutions and ancestral cultural while learning to speak English for communication, and participating in the political and economic life. (Gordon in Meister, 1974:91)

The Roman Catholic Church in the United States has been considered a monolithic subculture. This project will provide evidence of the persistence of both Americanization and ethnic cultural pluralism in the Catholic Church today, through research of the history of three Polish Language Juridical National Parishes, and other relevant contemporary documents. The Roman Catholic Church formulated and implemented a plan of Americanization in the early 1850's. This was to alleviate the fears of United States government officials and the Know-Nothing Party. The effect of this fear of the powers of the Pope over Catholics residing in the United States resulted in the reduction of cultural pluralism within the Catholic Church. Americanization to later arriving east European immigrants meant English language, and German or Irish hierarchy.

> "… the highest rank of Polish priests held in the hierarchy was that of monsignor. Of the sixty-nine bishops of the American Church in 1886, thirty-five bishops, archbishops, and cardinals were Irish by birth or descent, fifteen were German, eleven were French origin, five were English stock, and the remaining three were Dutch, Scots, and Spanish origin. Of these the Irish and the Germans formed a solid front against Polish demands to liberalize the definition of the Church in America." (Kuniczak, 1978:118)

In their overzealousness for the Roman Catholic Church to be accepted as an American institution, the hierarchy and many clergy attempted to force the immigrants to change their traditional manner of celebrating traditional feast days, the sacraments, and customs accompanying them. Many later arriving immigrants, found the adjustments to America too difficult to sustain without the moral support of the Roman Catholic Church, after being denied the sacraments in their own language. They were leaving the fold, not because they no longer believed in the faith, nor because they could not participate in the Mass, which was said in Latin, equally unintelligible to all but the most highly educated, but because the Catholic Church in America was not fulfilling their ethnic needs. (McAvoy 1970: 299-331)

John Carroll of Maryland was installed as bishop of Baltimore in 1790. Although frequently referred to as the first American Bishop, his position was ambiguous in breadth of his jurisdiction and the powers of authority. Under his charge were 25 priests and their parishes to which Bishop John Carroll held title. His jurisdiction was not over the 21 missions in California founded by the Franciscan Father Junipero Serra along the El Camino Real. These parishes were under the authority of the Bishop of Spain. Similarly Bishops in France, Ireland, Germany, Poland, and other countries continued to control their mission parishes in the Americas.

Not until June 29, 1908 had the Catholic Church in the United States been officially removed from Mission status under the jurisdiction of the Roman Congregation for the Propagation of the Faith, but Juridical National Parishes remained under the protection of this Congregation.

Ignoring the protected status of these Juridical National Parishes, the hierarchy persisted in its plan to Americanize the Catholic Church in the United States.

"… Irish Catholic bishops whose lack of understanding of Slavic immigrants expressed itself in a demand for instant 'Americanization' of Polish parishes. That meant that parishes organized by the Polish clergy, and churches built with hard earned Polish money, were to be turned over to Irish Pastors. This meant that sermons would be preached in English, which the immigrants could seldom understand and that all traces of Polish ceremonials, liturgical language, and discipline had to be abolished. This was too much even for the religious peasant immigrants. The community revolted." (Kuniczak, 1978: 118)

This precipitated the only lasting schism in the Roman Catholic Church in America. The "national" parish under the direct jurisdiction of the Holy See is not to be confused with the Polish National Catholic Church which was declared schismatic by Rome, soon after its founding in 1889 by Bishop Hodur. The schism is not of relevance to my paper, but rather that it reflected the intense feelings and actions of the Polish people that persist today.

In the midst of all this turmoil emerged the Juridical National Parish. This is an official ecclesiastically sanctioned church with members whose predominant language if other than English and whose ancestry is that same language, i.e. German, Polish, Italian, Spanish, Slovak, unified under the authority of the Society for the Propagation of the Faith, guided by the bishops in the continental United States but protected from annihilation by having direct recourse to the Holy See in Rome. It is used synonymously with language parish, national parish, and personal parish. It has no geographic boundaries of jurisdiction with many directives and limitations on membership. (Nuesse and Harte, 1959: 154-175)

The basic assumption was, that the role of these Juridical National Parishes would be one of gradual Americanization of the immigrants and facilitation of the Americanization of their children. There was the expectation that the language parishes would disappear with the second generation American born. Little research can be found on this subject as Milton M. Gordon states in Assimilation in American Life:

"Regrettably however to my knowledge, we do not have demographic trend studies of the "national" parish as a phenomenon in Roman Catholicism which would provide clues to its changing role and functions, or studies of particular "national" parish or group of such parishes through the crucial transition from the period of dominance of the first generation to that of the native born second and third generations as adults. Clearly the "national" parish will have its greatest attraction for the immigrant himself, who has not yet mastered the English tongue, and who brings with him his internalized cultural norms from Europe.

To what extent the second and third generation Italians, Poles, Slovaks, etc. have remained within the "national" parish is unknown in any strict quantitative sense, although informal observation would lead one to believe that there is a rapid falling away from the juridical "national" parish on the part of the American born Catholic, particularly if he is socially mobile and moves to a higher class area of second or third settlement, who then tends to take his place in the regular "territorial" parish. Certainly the policy of the church itself is not to foster nationality communalism any longer than is necessary." (1964; 197)

The "territorial" parish is the normal and preferred basis for the external organization of the Catholic population. Membership in a certain parish is determined by residence within officially prescribed boundaries. (Nuesse and Harte 1959: 84-88) A parish can be established prior to the construction of a church building. Frequently members of nearby parishes will request their own church located in their area for reasons of a growing population, prohibitive distances for an increasing number of people and occasionally for a "language" parish to serve the predominant membership living in a prescribed area. The latter however is not a Juridical National Parish.

I propose to study the actual cultural role of three Michigan Polish Juridical National Parishes at their formation, during a time of crises between the forces of Americanization and cultural pluralism, and the present: St. Albertus in Detroit, St. Mary of Czestochowa in rural Dwight Township, and All Saints in Flint. Today, these Juridical National Parishes remain vital. American born parishioners, of Polish descent, still live amid the same conflicts between Americanization forces and cultural pluralism.

Since there is no basic disagreement of doctrinal beliefs, Polish ethnicity becomes a dominant factor in the maintenance of these three parishes. The substitution of the word "parish" for "family" makes the following a workable definition for this project. "Ethnicity is a distinct group identification based on perceived similarities within a group, self-labeling in group terms, and patterned distinction of values, customs, and rituals of family life." (Zinn, 1980: 49)

These three parishes arouse during the unique, early, but vague formation of the American culture along pluralistic lines. Bruce Biever defines culture as (1) patterned behavior, (2) shared reality, (3) setting norms, (4) determining attitudes, (5) specifying behavior, (6) developing through group interaction (conscious learning and unconscious imitation), (7) a constantly changing and cumulative process, and (8) uniquely human activity. (Biever, 1965: 52-61)

Parish life today in St. Albertus, St. Mary of Czestochowa, and All Saints more closely resembles the "territorial" parish in the United States than the churches in Poland, while maintaining Polish traditions, ceremonies, liturgies, and services in the Polish language.

St. Albertus in Detroit was founded in 1872 at the request of Polish speaking

immigrants in the surrounding area before the official sanction of the Juridical National Parish. Early in its history, St. Albertus was embroiled in controversy, frequently referred to as the "Kolasinski Affair." This crisis had historical significance for the whole Roman Catholic Church in America. Today St. Albertus parishioners are deeply involved in an ethnic renewal program called the "Service of Tradition" inspired by the Second Vatican Council and Synod 69.

St Mary's of Czestochowa was founded in 1902, one of the first Juridical National Parishes in Michigan, located in rural Dwight Township. From 1978 to March of 1981, St. Mary's parishioners were in direct conflict with the presiding bishop resulting in civil court action. A restraining order from the court delayed the momentous decision to merge St. Mary's with a territorial parish near by in Kinde, St. Edwards, until the new bishop was instated. The new bishop has made allowances for the re-establishment of Polish traditions and use of the Polish language at Mass and other services.

All Saints in Flint was founded in 1910 after the precedent of the Juridical National Parish status was firmly established in the United States. All Saints while having internal personality confrontations, did not have major problems of a legal or hierarchical nature. Having multinational composition early it its development, fluctuations occurred when other ethnic groups became large enough to warrant the establishment of other Juridical National Parishes. The continuing role has been one of fostering "Cultural Pluralism" throughout All Saints' history.

The Triple Melting Pot

The theory of the "Triple Melting Pot" proposed by Will Herberg in his book, Protestant – Catholic – Jew, regards American society as intrinsically pluralistic, but fails to comprehend the ethnic pluralism still in evidence within the Roman Catholic Church in the United States today.

> The Catholic community today is one of the three great "melting pots' or, population "pools," into which America is divided. Within the Catholic community the innumerable ethnic elements that made up the immigrant church during the nineteenth and early twentieth century are being gradually amalgamated and a new type of American Catholic, rather along the Irish-American model, is emerging … It is still possible to find in an American town a whole array of "ethnic" Catholic churches – an Irish church (St. Patrick's), a French-Canadian (Sacre Coeur), an Italian (Our Lady of Carmel), a Hungarian (St. Stephen's), a Croation (St. Cyril and Methodius), a German (St. Boniface's) – but these churches are now usually English speaking and quite mixed in their membership. It is still possible to find survivals of the many diverse patterns of Catholic life and worship that more than a century of immigration brought to these shores but merely as survivals; here, too, there

has emerged an American pattern along the Irish-American lines into which what remains of the onetime diversity is being absorbed. There are those who see in this continuing dissolution of the "national" groups a serious weakening of the church but there are others who point out that this process is not only inevitable but is precisely the way in which the Catholic Church in America ceased to be foreign and has become an American institution. (Herberg 1955: 157-158)

Herberg continues to produce evidence that he believes supports the contention that the Catholic Church has become American in nature and that the need for "National" parishes has disappeared. Near the end of Chapter VII "Catholicism in America" he states: "… As we have stressed more than once American Catholicism has successfully negotiated the transition from a foreign church to an American religious community. It is now part of the American Way of Life." (Herberg 1955: 160)

As one will note in succeeding pages of this paper, the essential material proffered by Herberg as evidence of the changes in the Catholic Church are not as dramatic as he portrays and he does not adequately define "American." While saying that the Catholic Church is becoming American he conversely states: "The Catholic Church in America continues Irish in temper, tradition, and leadership." The Polish Juridical National Parishioners do not consider "Irish" to be "the American Way." They have fought and are continuing to fight to retain the ethnic character of their individual parishes although differing in degree.

The Unmeltable Ethnics

In the book, The Sociology of the Parish, edited by C. J. Nuesse and Thomas J. Harte, functions of the parish are discussed. A brief reference to fulfilling ethnic needs was introduced on page ten.

> It has often been the case in the United States, that the parish has served as a principal rallying point for an ethnic group, and that through this group or otherwise it has become, unwittingly perhaps, an organ of the group or of a class in the community. (Nuesse and Harte, eds. 1950: 10)

Illustrations of the church as a rallying point for the ethnic groups appear throughout the history of the Roman Catholic Church in America, often erupting in internal conflicts.

> In the early decade of the nineteenth century French and Irish openly argued over the control of St. Peter's Church in New York. Ostensibly the issue centered around the authority of parish trustees, but national prejudices were so intermingled with the trustee debate that it was difficult to separate the two.

> The Germans were the next group to challenge the hegemony of the parish. Their general complaint was that the Irish exercised an "undue influence" in church affairs … . They were afraid that after building their own Church, some later bishop, unsympathetic to Germans, might deprive them of it. When the Irishman John Hughes was appointed as Dubois's successor, the fears of the Germans became more real, and conflict inevitably emerged. (Dolan 1975: 89)

To a large extent histories and sociological studies of the Roman Catholic Church in the -United States recognize the Irish influence in internal affairs and the use of the Church to assimilate into the American way of life.

The Church had been first organized on a firm basis under the leadership of the Irish-American bishop, John Carroll. Its intellectual leadership was taken over in 1820 by the Irish born bishop, John England. By 1840, another Irishman, Archbishop Hughes of New York, had become not merely the most determined and forceful Churchman, but the outstanding man of his race in the country, a position he occupied for a quarter of a century. Their problem was that of building a Church in an ever-changing country with a constantly shifting population. Their flock was basically loyal but exasperatingly willful. It could not have been otherwise with hordes of famishing immigrants flooding the ports year after year, fighting for their very existence and clawing their way upwards for a place in the American sun … .

Dr. Carroll and later Dr. England found the diplomatic approach most rewarding in their time. But during the thirties and on into the late fifties racism under the names of Nativism or Knownothingism found its target in the increasing numbers of Irish immigrants. It was not a movement that appealed to Americans generally, but it became most violent in the centers were where immigrants, particularly the Irish, were in the highest concentration. Primarily, it was based on fear – fear that the immigrants were becoming a threat to the livelihood of Americans, but in the case of the Catholic Irish, latent bigotry, a colonial heritage which had been pushed into the background, revived in full fury in many of the eastern cities … .

The American Civil War (1861-1865) brought an end to violent expression of antipathy to the Irish immigrants. They had fought well in the Federal armies for the preservation of the Union. They had shown themselves good citizens and true upholders of American democratic ideals. They and their descendents were now a really substantial force in the New America. They, who had been so often in conflict with the law, in the rough-shod years of the country's development, now emerged as the custodians of the law. In the process, they developed a dynamic Church of great vitality. If that Church was a focal point for them and a source of great moral strength, it was of their own building, and it also provided their children with the education which enabled them to enter fully into the affairs of the nation. Many of these children they gave back to it, to become its servants and leaders … .

By 1870 … The customs, ideals and general outlook of the Church had now been established as a tradition. It was an Irish tradition with a lesser Germanic admixture. When the tide of immigration increased in the last quarter of century from Canada, France, Poland, other continental countries and finally Italy, its Catholic content came rather as an augmentation to the Church in America, whose broad characteristics had already been defined … . (Egan, 1968: 18-20)

It is this definition of the Catholic Church in America that was fought at St. Albertus parish in Detroit particularly during the "Kolasinski Affair," discussed in detail under that subtitle in this paper. Again in 1979 to 1981, Bishop Reh of the Saginaw Diocese could not understand that the Polish parishioners were willing to risk excommunication to retain their Polish cultural traditions within the Catholic Church.

This research also supports Michael Novak's insights in the book, The Rise of the Unmeltable Ethnics. His perception of Americanization is vividly described by the internal reactions to this external pressure.

The eyes of others, Hegel noted, are mirrors in which we learn our own identity. The first eyes into which the immigrants from southern and eastern Europe looked were Nordic eyes, the eyes of "old Americans," or "nativists." The immigrants were made to feel, as Adamic records, like dung. Behind the eyes of the nativists, however, there appeared in the 1960s the eyes of intellectuals. Two forms of prejudice stamped the immigrants. Both had a peculiar "northern" quality: one was racial, the other "progressive." According to one view, it was his race and religion that made the southern European inferior. According to the other, it was his social and political backwardness. The first bigotry drove the ethnics to the Democratic party. The second is tempting them toward the Republicans.

… many descendants of immigrants for many years withered into silence about their identity. Many suppressed the instincts of their flesh, the impulses of their sensibilities, and perhaps even the signals from their genes. (Teachers made Italian boys sit on their hands all morning long, to make them stop gesticulating.) A great many try desperately to be all alike, to look the way Americans do in the magazines, and movies, and streets: to make it, to pass.

Be warned. There is less and less reluctance about letting go. The days of racial and political bias against the ethnics are drawing to a close. (Novak, 1972: 78-79)

The Roman Catholic Church tried to mold its image into that of a Nativist American Institution. In its efforts it had to fight two labels, one of inferiority because of its ethnic members, the other, the Church of the laboring classes. The language parishes were interfering with this process.

The Irish were closer in culture, language and racial identification with the English and Nordic heritage so their assimilation although frequently stormy did not have the same tremendous suppression that was felt by the southern and eastern European immigrants. The bias against the ethnics may be diminishing but is not disappearing as the events at St. Mary Czestochowa reveal.

Methodology

Early histories of the Roman Catholic Church in North America were examined in order to determine the applicability of dominant sociological theories of Assimilation, Triple Melting Pot, and Cultural Pluralism. The histories of three representative Polish Juridical National Parishes were studied in an attempt to discern the role and possible role changes the parishes played in fulfilling the ethnic needs of their members. County census data, church registrations, and contribution envelope distribution were used to establish the ethnic ancestral composition of past and present parishioners. Newspaper and church publications were used in an attempt to define the roles of the hierarchy, clergy and members of all three parishes. Interviews of the respective pastors and parishioners were conducted to elaborate on the viability of church life.

Much published material is available for St. Albertus because it was the first Polish Church in Detroit, the largest city in Michigan. Although the years have colored the history they have also clarified some misunderstandings. In addition to the books, copies of original newspaper reports and recent articles reviewing past events and analyzing the changes taking place at St. Albertus abound. Telephone interviews were conducted with Reverend Joseph Matlenga present pastor of St. Albertus, and Lawrence Chominski, a parishioner who also wrote historical commentaries about St. Albertus Parish and Polish Traditions for the newspaper, The Citizen. In addition to serving on the Liturgical Committee for implementing the "Service of Tradition."

Lawrence Chominski played a large role in informing the Polish Community of the history making events that were occurring at St. Mary of Czestochowa in Dwight Township.

No books were available for St. Mary of Czestochowa. Original documents, including deeds to the land, state and county records, declaration of National status, letters, and decrees from clergy and hierarchy; including acknowledgements of receipt of correspondence from the Vatican were examined for indications of the role of this National Parish. Interviews were conducted with members of the parish. Especially important were interviews conducted with Ralph Majeski, the president of the Parish Council when the decree was issued by Bishop Reh that St. Mary of Czestochowa Parish was going to be suppressed. Ralph Majeski later headed the committee to retain their ethnic status, language, and traditions. Local newspaper coverage was broad and frequently made headlines in this small rural community. St. Mary of Czestochowa made historically significant moves it its defense of ethnicity.

All Saints seemingly more an international parish, still retains its Polish ethnic character. The 25th Year History of All Saints provided insight into this strange combination. The whole book including many advertisements were written in both Polish and English, while the participants in the Silver Jubilee Festivities included last names of fourteen nationalities and an international program. List of parishioners and advertisers were multi-ethnic but with predominantly identifiable Polish last names. Interviews were conducted with Reverend Anthony Majchrowski, present pastor, Mrs. Jenny Ferrara, the secretary and other presently active members of All Saints Parish.

Different degrees of assimilation and ethnic cultural pluralism for each parish are reported. Conclusions were drawn by comparing the roles of the parishes historically demographically, and following with trilateral correspondence analysis.

2. Early History of the Roman Catholic Church in the United States

The Second Vatican Council

When the first Catholic missionaries came to the North American Continent, they answered to the authority of the Bishops in their native countries. Father John Carroll became the first American Bishop in 1784 in the capacity of Superintendent of the American Catholic Missions, and was installed as Prelate in Baltimore, Maryland. His jurisdiction was to cover the entire mission territory of the American Church. With the wave of immigrants after 1840, from Poland, Italy and other south and east European countries, came priests who spoke the language of their flocks. Recognizing the lack of Priests, the divisiveness of non-localized control, organizational problems and trusteeism, in addition to the urgency of the loss of membership, succeeding bishops encouraged the foreign countries to continue sending priests to the United States with the reassurance that the priests' loyalties would remain with the Bishops of their native lands.
(Nuesse and Harte 1950: 45-48)

Pope Leo XIII was in regular contact with the presiding bishops about the existing problems in America. In a letter to Cardinal Gibbons dated 1898, the Pope expressed concern that the Catholic Church in the United States under the guise of Americanization was being contaminated by Protestant dogma. (McAvoy, 1970: 331)

> The letter began with a statement that his letter was a witness of affection but the Pope wanted to list some matters to be reproved and corrected, and that he wrote to end certain contentions. Gibbons, he said, was aware that certain doctrines had been introduced concerning christian life in connection with the publication of the biography of Father Hecker, especially in the translation. These doctrines advocated changes not only in methods of teaching the doctrines of the Church but even in the "Deposit of Faith," as

an indulgence to modern life and discoveries. Such changes in doctrine were contrary to the decrees of the council of the Vatican. Further discipline must be made by the church, not by individuals. The Pope specified certain special doctrines to which the name "Americanization" had been attached.

1. The rejection of external guidance and dependence, instead on the internal guidance of the Holy Spirit;
2. the extolling of natural virtues above supernatural virtues;
3. a distinction between active and passive virtues and the preference of active virtues, where the Pope said, all virtues were active;
4. the rejection of the evangelical virtues and vows of religious life as passive virtues;
5. the adoption of new ways to bring converts into the church.

New changes must be made under the direction of the local bishop and be accompanied by the wise observance of the sacred ceremonies and by good lives. The Pope added by this condemned "Americanism" he did not mean the characteristics of the American people. He also said, that if the reproved doctrines were taught in America, he was sure that the American bishops would reject them. (McAvoy, 1970: 332-333)

Cardinal Gibbons wrote an acceptance letter to the Pope in which he stated that no "educated" Catholic held the condemned doctrines. (McAvoy, 1970: 334)

Cardinal Gibbons, Archbishop Ireland, Bishop Spalding, and Bishop John Keane of the Catholic University were the leaders of those who sought to assimilate the incoming foreign Catholics in order to preserve the unity of the American Church against the disruptive strain of nationalism, and to allay the prejudice that the Catholic Church was a foreign institution, not amenable to American life. (Nuesse and Harte, 1950: 590)

Among the more conservative bishops were, Archbishop Alemany of San Francisco, who urged that priests knowing the language of newcomers should be placed in their parishes, also that all priests should learn two languages; Archbishop Corrigan of New York, Bishop McQuaid of Rochester, and other German bishops wanted the allocation of bishops and priests based on the number of the group in the population. (Nuesse and Harte, 1950: 59-62)

I was unable to determine which bishops designed the concept of the "national parish, of which Gordon speaks as 'a more modest step' that turned out in retrospect to have been an inspired middle ground position." (1964: 217) In an effort to stem the tide of immigrants leaving the fold, this inspired compromise received ecclesiastical sanction. It was hoped that the "national" parish would unify the Catholic Church in America, if all the already existing "language" churches could be unified under the authority of the Propagation of the Faith, guided by the bishops in the continental United States but protected from annihilation by having direct recourse to the Holy See in Rome.
(Nuesse and Harte, 1959: 154-175)

The American Roman Catholic Church was officially established in 1908 with the Territorial Parish as the preferred basis for external organization. Its boundaries are determined by its location. Some parishes encompass a few city blocks while others in rural areas may take in the whole county. On the other hand the "juridical national" parish emphasizes the language of the individual member.

The threads of what is American, what is Catholic and what is ethnicity are all intricately interwoven into the fabric which makes a Polish-American Catholic. The definitions, interpretations, and evaluations of these factors all contribute to the complexity of this analysis.

Contrary to Herberg's statement in his chapter on Catholicism:

> ... Its story is that of a foreign Church or rather a conglomeration of foreign churches, recruited from the successive waves of overseas immigrants, finally emerging into one of the three great 'American religions.' This remarkable transformation of a group socially and culturally alien into a thoroughly American religious community provides a significant clue to the inner history of Catholicism in the United States. (1960:13)

The establishment of the "national" parish is indicative of some of the actually tumultuous history. The "national" parish did not disappear, as expected, but was transmuted by succeeding generations to fulfill their needs.

Since the status of "national" parish is of prime importance to the maintenance of ethnicity within the Roman Catholic Church in America, the rights and regulation of membership must be noted. The differences of culture and more significantly language of Catholic immigrant groups from the European continent necessitated these "language" parishes. The power to erect "national" parishes comes from the Holy See, written in the Code of Canon Law is protection from change without express approval of the Holy See. (Nuesse and Harte, 1950: 158) English- speaking immigrants and their children upon reaching the accepted age of majority, individually are free to leave the "national" parish and join the "territorial" parish within which they reside. There is a restriction to the membership in these "personal" parishes.

> Thus, an English-speaking Slovak immigrant may not join a Polish Church because he does not like his Slovak pastor; though he may have knowledge of Polish, he must choose between his Slovak parish and the territorial parish in which he lives. (Nuesse and Harte, 1950; 159)

The Juridical National Parish concept was clarified and regulations were redefined in 1897 and again in 1938. In most cases territorial parishes are maintained in the same area as "national" parishes with boundaries often overlapping. (Nuesse and Harte, 1950: 154)

The Second Vatican Council

The directives and suggestions arising from The Second Vatican Council were used to support opposite positions taken by two presiding bishops in recent years. Archbishop John Cardinal Dearden of Detroit encouraged Father Joseph Matlenga in 1972 and 1973 to restore the traditional Polish liturgies, services and celebrations at St. Albertus using the directives of the documents as the basis for his actions. On the other hand Bishop Reh in 1979 through 1981 fought the retention of ethnic art, structure, traditions and language at St. Mary of Czestochowa in Dwight Township with references and decrees that the "Polishness" of the parish was not in keeping with the recommendations from Vatican II Documents.

A close look at the writings of the Bishops at the Second Vatican Council reveals that both interpretations can be valid but that the emphasis on one section by Bishop Reh without consideration of the many other sections fostering cultural retention led to the controversy at St. Mary of Czestochowa.

To support his "Suppression of St. Mary of Czestochowa Parish" Bishop Reh used from the Vatican II Documents, "The Decree on the Bishops Pastoral Office in Church: Chapter 2 – Bishops and Their Particular Churches or Dioceses, Section 16":

> In exercising his office of father and pastor, a bishop should stand in the midst of his people as one who serves. Let him be a good shepherd who knows his sheep and whose sheep know him. Let him be a true father who excels in the spirit of love and solicitude for all and to whose divinely conferred authority all gratefully submit themselves.

Let him so gather and mold the whole family of his
flock that everyone conscious of his own duties, may
live and work in the communion of love.

To accomplish these things effectively a bishop,
"ready for every good work" (2 Timothy 2:21) and
"enduring all things for the sake of the chosen ones"
(2 Timothy 2:10), should arrange his life in such a
way as to accommodate it to the needs of the time.
(Abbott, ed., 1966: 408)

In his interpretation Bishop Reh saw the merging of the two
parishes, St. Edward and   St. Mary of Czestochowa, into a new
modern parish with a new name, as a means to unify the Catholic
Family of God in the area and encourage Americanization of the
Polish-American members.

Archbishop Dearden proceeded to emphasize other sections of
the Vatican II Documents, regarding St. Albertus Parish. From the
"Constitution on the Sacred Liturgy Chapter I General Principles for
the Restoration and Promotion of the Sacred Liturgy, part (d) Norms
for Adapting the Liturgy to the Genius and Traditions of Peoples":

37. Even in the liturgy, the Church has no wish to impose a
rigid uniformity in matters which do not involve the faith or
the good of the whole community. Rather she respects and
fosters the spiritual adornments and gifts of the various
races and peoples. Anything in their way of life that is not
indissolubly bound up with superstition and error, she
studies with sympathy and, if possible, preserves intact.
Sometimes in fact she admits such things into the liturgy
itself, as long as they harmonize with its true authentic spirit.

38. Provided that the substantial unity of the Roman rite is maintained, the revision of liturgical books should allow for legitimate variations and adaptations to different groups, regions, and peoples, especially in mission lands. Where opportune, the same rule applies to the structuring of rites and the devising of rubrics.

39. Within the limits set by the typical editions of the liturgical books, it shall be for the competent territorial ecclesiastical authority mentioned in Article 22, Section 2, to specify adaptations, especially in the case of the administration of the sacraments, the sacramentals, processions, liturgical language, sacred music, and the arts, but according to the fundamental norms laid down in this Constitution.

40. In some places and circumstances, however, an even more radical adaptation of the liturgy is needed and entails greater difficulties.

Therefore:

(1) The competent territorial ecclesiastical authority mentioned in Article 22, Section 2, must, in this matter, carefully and prudently consider which elements from the traditions and genius of individual peoples might appropriately be admitted into divine worship. Adaptations which are judged to be useful or necessary should then be submitted to the Apostolic See, by whose consent they may be introduced.
(2) To ensure that adaptations are made with all necessary circumspection, the Apostolic See will grant power to this same territorial ecclesiastical authority to permit and to direct, as the case requires, the necessary preliminary experiments over a determined period of time among certain groups suited for the purpose.
(3) Because liturgical laws often involve special difficulties with respect to adaptation, particularly in mission lands, men who are experts in these matters must be employed to formulate them. (Abbott, ed., 1966: 151-152)

From the same Liturgy document,

Chapter VI Sacred Music Section 114:

> 114. The treasure of sacred music is to be preserved and fostered with very great care. Choirs must be diligently promoted, especially in cathedral churches; but bishops and other pastors of souls must be at pains to ensure that, whenever the sacred action is to be celebrated with song, the whole body of the faithful may be able to contribute that active participation which is rightly theirs, as laid down in Articles 28 and 30. (Abbott, ed., 1966: 171-172)

From the same Liturgy document, Chapter VII Sacred Art and Sacred Furnishings, Section 122 and 123:

> 122. Very rightly the fine arts are considered to rank among the noblest expressions of human genius. This judgment applies especially to religious art and to its highest achievement, which is sacred art. By their very nature both of the latter are related to God's boundless beauty, for this is the reality which these human efforts are trying to express in some way. To the extent that these works aim exclusively at turning men's thoughts to God persuasively and devoutly, they are dedicated to God and to the cause of His greater honor and glory.
>
> Holy Mother Church has therefore always been the friend of the fine arts and has continuously sought their noble ministry, with the special aim that all things set apart for use in divine worship should be truly worthy, becoming, and beautiful, signs and symbols of heavenly realities. For this purpose, too, she has trained artists. In fact, the Church has, with good reason, always reserved to herself the right to pass judgment upon the arts, deciding which of the works of artists are in accordance with faith, piety, and cherished traditional laws, and thereby suited to sacred purposes.

123. The Church has not adopted any particular style of art as her very own; she has admitted fashions from every period according to the natural talents and circumstances of peoples, and the needs of the various rites. Thus, in the course of the centuries, she has brought into being a treasury of art which must be very carefully preserved. The art of our own days, coming from every race and region, shall also be given free scope in the Church, provided that it adorns the sacred buildings and holy rites with due honor and reverence. It will thereby be enabled to contribute its own voice to that wonderful chorus of praise in honor of the Catholic faith sung by great men in times gone by. (Abbott, ed., 1966: 174-175)

Then from part II Some Problems of Special Urgency, Chapter II, The Proper Development of Culture, Introduction section 53:

53. It is a fact bearing on the very person of man that he can come to an authentic and full humanity only through culture, that is, through the cultivation of natural goods and values. Wherever human life is involved, therefore, nature and culture are quite intimately connected.

The word "culture" in its general sense indicated all those factors by which man refines and unfolds his manifold spiritual and bodily qualities. It means his effort to bring the world itself under his control by his knowledge and his labor. It includes the fact that by improving customs and institutions he renders social life more human both within the family and in the civic community. Finally, it is a feature of culture that throughout the course of time man expresses, communicates, and conserves in his works great spiritual experiences and desires, so that these may be of advantage to the progress of many, even of the whole human family.

Hence it follows that human culture necessarily has a historical and social aspect and that the word "culture" often takes on a sociological and ethnological sense. It is in this sense that we speak of a plurality of cultures.

Various conditions of community living, as well as various patterns for organizing the goods of life, arise from diverse ways of using things, of laboring, or expressing oneself, of practicing religion, of forming customs, of establishing laws and juridical institutions of advancing the arts and sciences, and of promoting beauty. Thus the customs handed down to it form for each human community its proper patrimony. Thus, too, is fashioned the specific historical environment which enfolds the men of every nation and age and from which they draw the values which permit them to promote human and civic culture. (Abbott, ed., 1966: 259-260)

3. St. Albertus, Detroit's Oldest Polish Parish

A National Historic Site

St. Albertus, Detroit's first Polish parish, founded in 1872, has managed to reserve its ethnicity, as well as the traditional Catholic faith, while under the pressures of diocesan circumstances and of a changing urban community.

The founding pastor, Reverend Simon Wieczorck was high in determination but low in financial understanding, leading to the first confrontation with Bishop Borgess, whose position was originally one of judicial ambiguity. "Canonically, Bishop Borgess was only the administrator of the diocese, since the episcopal title was still held by the first bishop of Detroit until his death, December 30, 1971." (Swastek, 1972:36) His diocese was Michigan's entire Lower Peninsula with a Catholic population of approximately 150,000 in 1869. Eighty-eight priests served this ethnically diverse Catholic populace: "… thirty-nine Belgians, twenty-one Germans, nine Irishmen, six native-born Americans (including four Michiganders), five Frenchmen and two Poles." (Swastek, 1972:36) Bishop Lefevere before him administered the Diocese "in somewhat flexible financial and disciplinary manner," so Bishop Borgess, "schooled in orderly procedures in the Cincinnati Chancery" introduced an "efficiency program." (Swastek, 1972:37)

Swastek's commentary illuminates the reader:

> The introduction of this efficiency program did not contribute to Bishop Borgess' popularity either among the clergy or among the laity. He was represented as being 'cold, severe, caring little for social intercourse, always unbending.' In reality he was a man with a strong sense of duty, interested in promoting the welfare of the diocese as a whole, and not afraid to risk unpopular decisions designed to save the parishioners from the consequences of their own misjudgments or mistakes.

This last sentence sums up the initial tangled relations between Bishop Borgess and the Polish-Prussian founders of St. Albertus Parish between 1870 and 1873. Later chroniclers, lacking sufficient documentary evidence as well as discriminating judgment, have unjustly caricatured Bishop Borgess as a Pole-hater and an enemy of Polish education in Detroit.

As a matter of cold historical fact, Bishop Borgess was neither. His two confrontations with the founders and first pastor of St Albertus Parish, usually cited against him by Polish chroniclers relying uncritically on Fr. Kruszka's incomplete and one-sided presentation, actually reflect credit on the bishop's good judgment when the controversies are examined in their proper context and judged in the light of the bishop's surviving correspondence. (Swastek, 1972: 37)

Letters from Bishop Borgess reveal his caution in giving permission to the committee requesting the founding of a Polish Church. His main concerns were the ability of the parishioners to fulfill their financial obligations and the availability of Polish speaking priests from the Resurrectionist order. The committee moved ahead with purchasing land before Fr. Simon had assumed pastoral duties.

The first church building and rectory were completed but "not entirely to the satisfaction of the trustees who, in consequence, temporarily withheld the final payment called for by the terms of the contract." (Swastek, 1972:41) The Bishop ordered the committee to pay the debt and threatened punishment to the entire worshiping community, including excommunication. The matter was settled by the Parish taking out a loan to pay the architect, the architect posted a surety bond with Bishop Borgess, and the Bishop withdrew his threats but with a letter of caution warning Fr. Simon to submit all financial proposals before making any decisions. (Swastek, 1972:41)

Fr. Simon committed "an unpardonable disobedience" by allowing parishioners to contract and construct a church school which was subsequently foreclosed upon by the owner of the land. For this Father Simon was dismissed as pastor. But "Bishop Borgess in another show of compassion repurchased for the parish the foreclosed school parcel ..." (Swastek, 1972:45)

While Bishop Borgess seemed to be dealing rather harshly with the Polish parishioners, it was primarily for business mishaps not anything relevant to their ethnic backgrounds. The fact that Bishop Borgess was of German birth was coincidental to the confrontations: Swastek addresses this misunderstanding.

> The prominent and numerous German participation in the dedication cast doubt on subsequent allegations by some chroniclers that St. Albertus Church was founded as a reaction against German discrimination toward Polish members of their congregation who were supposedly required to occupy certain specified pews in the church.

> (Swastek, 1972:39)

The more likely reason for the establishment of St. Albertus was the numerical increase of Polish immigrants to the Detroit area, their desire to be ministered to in their Polish language, and to engage in traditionally Polish religious events.

St. Albertus, St. Alberts, St. Adalberts

Various spellings all referring to St. Albertus have been recorded in the histories of both St. Mary of Czestochowa and All Saints. The source of this confusion came in the translation from Polish. Swastek explains:

> But before any further repercussions of the bishop's changing attitude toward Fr. Simon came to the surface, the new pastor of St. Albertus began to busy himself with the minutiae of parochial administration. With the

church blessed and the parishioners spiritually renewed by a mission, Fr. Simon began the parish register of births, and marriages inscribed in a neat and distinctive script: Registrum Paptisatorum et Matrimonii in Ecclesia Sti. Adalberti ... Here Fr. Simon used St. Wojciech's confirmation name, Adalbertus, which became, in its anglicized form of St. Adalbert, the official title of thirty-three of the thirty-four churches dedicated to this saint in the United States.

Only Detroit's congregation adopted St. Albertus as its English title for some reason that remains obscure to this day. During the early decades of the parish, it was known in Detroit newspapers and City Directories, and in the Catholic Directories as well as on the parish's stationery and in the chancery records, as St. Albert's Church. In fact when Bishop Borgess recorded the dedication of the church in the chancery ledger under the year 1872 in terse Latin, he wrote: "On the 14th of July, I blessed the new church under the title and invocation of St. Albert in the City of Detroit." Saints Albert and Adalbert are two different persons; and the name of neither one is a correct English equivalent for the Czech Vojtech or its polonized version Wojciech. But at this date it is perhaps too late to make the correction. (Swastek, 1972:40)

Indications of Another Crisis

After rescinding his order of June 7, 1873, closing the church "for every Catholic divine service of any kind" in a spirit of compassion Bishop Borgess assigned Rev. Theodore Gieryk. Under his direction in full compliance with the previous directives issued by the Bishop, St. Albertus' first elementary school was completed.

Father Gieryk, now recognized as the founder of The Polish Roman Catholic Union, was somewhat visionary. After a convention to organize "to promote the betterment of the Poles in America," he issued a manifesto.

> … appealing in the name of the new organization to all Polish Catholics on behalf of our "widows and orphans," the unemployed hungry men, and the unschooled children, to put aside their differences (some of them artificially generated by the partitioning powers). In closing, Fr. Gieryk called on the Poles in the name of American liberty and democracy to create a united Polish front for the common good, "by majority vote" to which a dissident minority would be bound to accede. (Swastek, 1972:50)

Another achievement of Father Gieryk was The Polish Catholic Gazette (Gazeta Polska Katolicka) which was brought to Detroit to publish the news for the Union of Polish Catholics. It was the "eighth Polish newspaper founded in the United States and the first avowedly Catholic one." Fr. Gieryk resigned his pastorate to devote more time to The Union of Polish Catholics later renamed The Polish Roman Catholic Union. But this was only to last three months, for at the Union's third convention he was not re-elected to its presidency.

Following Fr. Gieryk as pastor of St. Albertus as Father Alfons Dombrowski who "displayed considerable disdain for what he perceived to be the unhealthy moral condition of his Polish Parish." (Orton, 1981:22) but ended up being dismissed from his pastoral duties due to a personal scandal. A summary of reports appearing in the Evening News radio programs was written by Lawrence D. Orton in the book, Polish Detroit and the Kolasinski Affair.

> But as Dombrowski's pastorate wore on, the parishioners as well as the bishop came to discover an even more "unhealthy moral condition" in the pastor than he had discerned in the congregation. In 1879 complaints against the priest reached the bishop with mounting frequency. He was accused of denying confession and communion to impoverished members who had failed to pay their parish dues and of "drinking and playing cards" on Sunday evenings in public places. Worse, on 8 September the Evening News disclosed a far more serious charge. It reported that an irate Pole had awakened Circuit Court Commissioner J. A. Randall in the middle of the night to press charges against Dombrowski for seducing his wife and being the father of her recently born child. Not only had the couple been married only six months, but just prior to the marriage the woman, identified as Julia Kuhla, had worked as a domestic in the priest's house. Kuhla swore out a warrant against Dombrowski, but when the priest agreed to pay $1,100.00 in damages, Kuhla dropped the suit. The scandal prompted Bishop Borgess to summon the accused priest to the episcopal residence the next day, 9 September. After a "summary trial" that apparently satisfied the bishop that the charges were based on fact, he

removed Dombrowski as pastor of St. Albertus's Church. This was only the first of Dombrowski's troubles. When he failed to vacate the rectory immediately, a mob of Poles besieged him there on the evening of 10 September and attempted to evict him by force. The priest took refuge at a friend's house and, angered by the threat to his person, swore out a complaint against three of the trustees, whom he accused of being the ringleaders. Dombrowski remained in Detroit for several weeks and reportedly tried to bribe Mrs. Kuhla to sign a paper (in English, which she could not read) absolving him of the paternity claim. The ruse failed, and the unfortunate "von" Dombrowski left the city, and it is assumed, the priesthood as well. (Orton, 1981:23)

After serving two years as assistant to Father Dombrowski, Jan Wollowski was made pastor, but his handicap of having only one arm added to his burden of caring for a rapidly growing and still troubled parish. His moral character, however, was never under question.

Though the bishop did not provide a new assistant, Wollowski sought aid on his own within the diocese, often from the Czech Fr. Vaclav Tilek, who lived nearby. But among the parishioners the rumor persisted that Wollowski, because of his disability, was not able to celebrate Mass properly. Whatever his physical limitation, however, Wollowski, unlike his predecessor , was never faulted for not being "ultra Polish," and during his pastorage he fostered numerous Polish religious traditions, notably, the pasterka, or Christmas Eve midnight Mass. (Orton, 1981: 25)

The denial of the "pasterka" during the pastorate of the succeeding priest led to violence and bloodshed.

The Kolasinski Affair

Flamboyant Father Dominek Kolasinski precipitated the most far-reaching crisis in the history of St. Albertus Parish. Originally the conflict between Father Kolasinski and the parish elders was mainly financial called "trusteeism" in which the property and financial affairs of the parish were controlled by a board of lay people as was common in Europe, rather than the clergy with ownership in the name of the bishop as was and is customary in the United States.

The gravity of the crises between Bishop Caspar H. Borgess was not fully comprehended by the parishioners until Father Kolasinski was suspended as a priest and was asked to leave St. Albertus. The parishioners found it difficult to believe the allegations against Father Kolasinski. Their anger heightened when Rev. Josef Dabrowski (who was perceived by the parishioners as a rival of Father Kolasinski), was appointed temporary pastor.

Three periods can be identified in this explosive controversy. First, Father Kolasinski was dismissed from the pastorate on November 28, 1885 but did not vacate the rectory until April 5, 1886 after a civil court order was issued. This was the most volatile of the three time frames. (Orton, 1981)

Lawrence D. Orton in his book, Polish Detroit and the Kolasinski Affair gives a social-economic description of Detroit during this historic interval.

> ... The times were not good economically, and many of the most recent, unskilled immigrants had great difficulty in obtaining even irregular employment as day laborers. But they were members of "the finest Polish Church in America," and their pastor's elegant office and manner and his adherence to the ways of the

old country provided them with a sense of familiarity and security in this strange new land. Understandably, then, the news that the 'German" bishop, Caspar H. Borgess, had suspended "their" priest and directed him to leave the diocese brought consternation and anger to the Polish Parishioners. The ostensible reason for the pastor's removal (no formal charges were released by the bishop and no ecclesiastical investigation had been held), that Father Kolasinski had declined to submit the parish's financial records until they could be brought up to date, seemed of little consequence to the essentially peasant congregation and was hardly grounds to remove their adored pastor. Kolasinski's refusal to turn over the books provided an excuse to suspend a man whom the bishop had already decided to remove because of mounting charges of misappropriation and mismanagement of parish funds and allegation of moral turpitude. Details regarding this last charge, certainly the most inflammatory and damaging, came to light only later and fueled an already full-blown crisis. (Orton, 1981: 41)

Parishioners, a majority of them women, opposed the appointment of Father Josef Dabrowski, the minister to the Felicia Convent across the street from St. Albertus. After being attacked by angry attendant at only one Mass, Fr. Dabrowski never returned to St. Albertus Church to say Mass although he remained pastor for over a year and a half in name only. (Orton, 1981: 45)

Both English and Polish news coverage aggravated the situation by sensationalizing the "Polish Riots" that ensued during these months by exaggerating charges by the involved, except Bishop Borgess who avoided the discontented parishioners and journalists alike. Father Kolasinski engaged a lawyer, John Corliss to call upon Bishop Borgess and,

> ... to convey his client's willingness to turn over all parish financial records and answer all charges against him if a properly constituted ecclesiastical hearing were convened ...... A man not known to relent, he would give no hint of yielding to the Poles' wishes to see their priest reinstated. Instead on Friday, 4 December, the bishop promulgated an official decree of interdiction on St. Albertus's Church, banning all religious functions. The order was read in all the Catholic Churches of the city and had almost the same effect as excommunication, since it also closed the doors of these other churches to the "dissident" members of the proscribed parish. Though the interdiction was temporary, it was to remain in effect for almost nineteen months. (Orton, 1981: 48)

This interdict led directly to the "Bloody Polish Christmas Riot" (as the combined newspaper reports described it). (Swastek, 1973: 81) The "pasterka," fostered by Father Wollowski, the one-armed priest, was now denied to the parishioners on December 24, 1885.

The following is a combined synopsis of the two authors Orton and Swastek describing the tragic events of that holiday season. After being denied participation at the celebration of "Midnight Mass," "pasterka" "Shepherd's Mass," the ostracized followers of Father Kolasinski and opponents of Father Dabrowski dispersed after a minor skirmish. The began to reassemble in front of St. Albertus Church. "... by five o'clock a crowd estimated at eight hundred men, women and children, bright and clean in their holiday attire, had assembled about the church hoping that the doors would open to let them celebrate an early Christmas Mass ..." (Orton, 1981: 51) The crowd was estimated at several thousand by the time approved for Masses had passed. A decision was made "... to march to the Episcopal residence ... to appeal personally to the bishop for permission to hold Christmas services in their church." (Orton, 1981: 51)

Orton quotes the Evening News radio coverage of this assembly:

> There was little or no jabbering or demonstration. The faces wore an expression of extreme earnestness. They appeared to feel keenly the fact that while other church bells were ringing, other congregations were bowing before their altars and offering thanks to God, they stood crowded and shivering in the streets with their church cold and silent and with the frown of their bishop upon them ... The men were well dressed in the holiday garb of laborers and mechanics. The brilliant red shawls of the women gave a picturesque look to the otherwise somber appearance of the body. (Orton, 1981: 51)

Out of the thousands of marchers to arrive at the Bishop's residence close to nine o'clock, six were chosen to appeal to the Bishop for one Christmas Mass. The Bishop avoided the delegation and the crowd by going out the back way of the episcopate to say Mass at St. Joseph's German Church. The Poles followed undaunted in their desire for Mass, but were again rebuffed and physically blocked from entering St. Joseph's Church. (Orton, 1981: 51)

A reporter for the newspaper, The Free Press, captured well the mood of the Poles at this juncture.

Thus balked at every turn and with all their efforts useless, the homeless congregation realized fully that they were debarred entirely from observing the day according to their religious training and belief and it was at this point that women began to cry ... Their leaders, however, kept them well in hand so that there was no sign of a disturbance of the peace and so they marched back to the corner of St. Aubin Avenue and Fremont Street, reaching there about noon. Then the crowd slowly dispersed. (Orton, 1981: 52)

St. Albertus Church building was located on the corner of St. Aubin and Fremont but the crowd did not attempt to force entry to the church.

Father Kolasinski had at an earlier date said that among his critics were mostly saloon keepers that he had criticized for leading immigrants astray and doing business on Sundays. Now, the distraught, virtually excommunicated parishioners started regrouping in front of the "Saloon and grocery store owned by Jan Lemke and his sons, now identified as leaders of the Pro-Dabrowski faction." (Orton, 1981: 52) Verbal assaults and some objects were tossed at the house, then a fifteen year old youth ran up to the door and kicked the door.

> ... Almost immediately, the door opened and a man appeared holding a revolver. Although it was already quite dark, most sources suggested that he was Basil Lemke. Other men could be seen behind him in the doorway. Four shots were fired into the crowd. One struck Jan Lewicki just over the left eye, entering the brain and causing instant death. Another shot grazed a woman standing nearby. The police then forced an entrance into the house and arrested all the men inside, except for the elder Lemke, since no one would admit to the shooting.

The Lemkes later claimed that the first shots came from the crowd and that they had merely fired in self-defense.   The dead Pole, Jan Lewicki, was in his mid twenties and, though a member of St. Albertus' Parish, was not known to support either the Kolasinski or Dabrowski factions. (Orton, 1981: 52)

The second day of the Christmas season following the Bishop's rejection and the shooting, turmoil was intensified. A more unruly crowd than the first gathered around the church. The police were called but rather than containing the crowd, they only succeeded in shunting the Poles from one street to another while the numbers steadily grew. (Orton, 1981: 53)

In the aftermath of the shooting of Lewicki and the bishop's behavior on Christmas Day, there was an outpouring of criticism of Borgess by prominent Detroit lay Catholics. Most maintained that if he had displayed more flexibility and understanding of the people's feelings, the bloodshed probably could have been averted. One critic was quoted in the Evening News as saying, "It was certainly not upholding the sacerdotal dignity to retreat through the alleyway, when those poor people, through an excess of faith, called upon him to solicit some services in their church. The bishop ought to remember that it is far easier to drive people out of the church than to drive them back again." An editorial in the Evening Journal pointedly concluded that "there was no mob" of Poles on Christmas Day "until the bishop had left his residence by the alleyway without meeting either the committee of the petitioners or the petitioners themselves." (Orton, 1981: 54)

Bishop Borgess refused to see reporters and attempted to place the blame for the "Riots" and shootings on Father Kolasinski through Father Dempsey. On the other hand, Father Kolasinski charmed reporters with his gracious manner and fluent German.

Newspapers exaggerated the troubles in the Polish quarters of Detroit with reports of an increase in gun sales which upon investigation could not be corroborated by any gun stores. A Reverend Konstanty Domagalski was given permission to speak to reporters about substantiated wrong-doings of Reverend Kolasinski in Krakow, Poland. These accusations were denied through Kolasinski's attorney.

After three months Bishop Borgess began civil proceedings to evict Reverend Kolasinski from the rectory. Father Kolasinski appealed to Archbishop William Elder, in Cincinnati, whose jurisdiction included the Detroit Diocese. Kolasinski saw that he would eventually have to leave Detroit so he attempted to procure an exeat, a document releasing him from further obligations to the diocese.

Although Father Kolasinski vacated the rectory April 5, 1886, it was after April 9, 1886, that he left for the Dakota Territory. Militant supporters sought to regain St. Albertus Parish for Father Kolasinski from April 6, 1886 to December 7, 1888.

March 20, 1887, Bishop Borgess issued a formal declaration of excommunication, retroactive to December 1, 1885, of parishioners from St. Albertus Parish who participated in the riots and/or supported the reinstatement of Father Kolasinski. April 16, 1887, Bishop Borgess officially laid down the miter, and acceptance of which came on May 6, 1887. Nineteen months passed before a successor was named, these events were influential in setting the directions for Father Kolasinski's future.

Between December 8, 1888 and February 17, 1894:

> Father Kolasinski returned to Detroit without
> the bishop's authorization and on his own
> authority, erected two successive Polish
> churches not subject to local episcopal control
> and formed one of the largest Polish
> congregations in Detroit if not in Michigan.
> (Swastek, 1972: 74)

During his interim stay in the Dakota Territory, Kolasinski was not forgotten, for on December 9, 1888, his first day back in Detroit over three thousand Polish followers stood in cold and mud waiting for a word of encouragement.

After a brief meeting with Bishop Foley on December 15, 1888, in which Kolasinski was denied a rehearing, the decision to build an independent church free of episcopal authority was made by the Kolasinski followers, Kolasinski-ites. Not without external and internal conflicts, slanders, and misappropriations, the construction of the first maverick church began, named Sweetest Heart of Mary. The sentiments of the Kolasinski-ites were summed up by Frederick Reeder after his delivery of a formal document to Bishop Foley. "Bishop Foley ain't got hell in one pocket and heaven in the other anymore, and put Polacks in which pocket he likes." (Quoted by Orton, 1981: 95, from Sunday News, May 12, 1889, p. 2) Another indication of the fervor of the followers of Kolasinski, also the effects of the interdict and excommunication was the postponement of Baptisms, First Communions, and Weddings by Poles that were too Catholic to seek civil services or change religions. (Orton, 1981: 69-97)

Upon his return Father Kolasinski was officiating at twenty weddings each week. In less than a month "the treasurer of the ostracized flock, Kazimierz Nowak, announced that $17,000.00 had been raised in cash pledges toward a new church." (Orton, 1981: 95) Its membership was estimated between 12,000 individuals and 2,783 families but each family frequently had between seven and twelve children, making these estimates more convergent that a quick first glance indicates.

The second, a more conservative structure for the maverick flock was built just three blocks west of Sweetest Hear of Mary's and named St. Josaphat. In the same year, 1889, a fourth cornerstone for a territorial church was laid in West Detroit for St. Casmir's Church at Myrtle and Twenty-Third Streets.

The last church, St. Casmir's was to portray the meltability of ethnic Catholics into American Catholics.

> The dedication, in which representatives of all the city's loyal Catholic parishes and organizations took part, was staged primarily as an endorsement of the tribute to Bishop Foley and his policies since assuming control of the diocese eight months before. In his sermon Foley commended the harmonious spirit of Detroit's Catholics: "the faithful sons of Erin, the sturdy sons of Germany, the children of sunny France, the sons of Poland, and the liberty-loving children of our own dear republic ... All nationality is buried today, and we stand around this first stone as Catholics ... Here no bitter Czar rules; here is no raging lion to crush the sons of Erin. Here we are all freemen. All that is asked is that we be good citizens." The harmony of which the bishop spoke was achieved, however, largely by denying Kolasinski and his followers their place in the ceremonial procession. (Orton, 1981: 100)

Bishop Foley repeatedly tried to warn Kolasinski's followers that, "... not only was Kolasinski leading his people into religious deviation, but his ways were contrary to the ideals of the Poles newly adopted country." (Orton, 1981: 413) Despite the warnings, the Pastor of

St. Albertus in 1889 was loosing parishioners because his sermons were in a German dialect with little Polish, and these disgruntled Poles were turning to Sweetest Heart of Mary's. (Orton, 1981: 413)

Three years after its construction in 1892, the cornerstone at Sweetest Heart of Mary's was finally "blessed," but by a fake bishop, adding to the scandals of the "Kolasinski Affair." Kolasinski contacted the apostolate delegate to North America, Monsignor Francesco Satolli with hopes of realigning Sweetest Heart of Mary with the Holy See. Not until months later did the Monsignor consider reopening the Kolasinski case. (Orton, 1981: 125)

The second cathedral like church in Detroit was dedicated December of 1893 with over fifteen thousand devoted parishioners. For the first time in nine years "Pasterka" was celebrated in their own language, in their own church, Sweetest Heart of Mary. The economic picture was poor, unemployment was high, small houses were mortgaged, all to have a "Home" for their Polish Catholic traditions. (Orton, 1981: 126-127)

Internal political factions siding with Kolasinski and Bishop Foley aired their differences in secular newspapers again bringing the attention of Monsignor Satolli to the "Kolasinski Affair." Since over 15,000 souls were in jeopardy consideration of a reconciliation was imperative. Monsignor Donato Sbaretti became Monsignor Satolli's personal representative at hearings of the "Kolasinski Case."

The principal obstacle to Kolasinski's reinstatement, according to canonical law, was his decision to return to Detroit in 1888 and act as a priest in defiance of Foley's ruling. In his negotiations with Sbaretti, Kolasinski argued that, although Borgess had provided him with an exeat in April 1888, the bishop had failed to supply an ineat confirming his entrance into the Dakota diocese; therefore, under ecclesiastical law, Kolasinski had technically remained a subject of the Detroit Diocese during his absence. (Orton, 1981: 132)

Rather than close the church to services an agreement was made that Father Kolasinski would do penance for one week away from the parish and prior to his departure the Church would be officially blessed, the congregation reinstated to full communion under the Holy Father in Rome, and

> ... the schismatic priest (Father Kolasinski) would have to read his recantation in three languages – Polish, German and English – before his congregation. He also would have to make an annual accounting of his parish's financial affairs. It was reliably reported that Kolasinski acceded to these terms and that an agreement was signed on Saturday evening. (Orton, 1981: 138)

Expected opposition to his light penance came from Detroit clergy, who might have feared that Kolasinski's oratory skills and personal magnetism might charm away their "faithful" parishioners. Understandably, Bishop Foley was not voluntarily readmitting Father Kolasinski and his adherents voiced their displeasure.

One priest who asked to remain anonymous freely voiced his displeasure to a Free Press reporter and was bitter because "foreigners, and Italians" who "can hardly speak a word of English" and knew nothing of the affair, could impose a settlement. The priest suggested, not unlike Father Dorman earlier, that Sbaretti was acting to impress Rome and obtain a promotion. Another anonymous source called the settlement one of "the most scandalous things that has occurred in the history of American Catholicism," adding that, whatever Satolli ordered, "no amount of recantation will ever bring back to (Kolasinski) the respect of Catholics." A Catholic weekly, the Angelus, added its voice to the general discontent: "Every Catholic feels himself the subject of a personal outrage at this shocking surprise." (Orton, 1981: 139)

Father Kolasinski was not to be removed as pastor, but would have to submit to the authority of Bishop Foley. After an eloquent sermon on February 18, 1894, the subject, "The Transfiguration of Our Lord," Father Kolasinski was to read his apologies.

Then, with a sudden movement of his hand, he extracted several pages of manuscript from his vestments. His followers sensed that some momentous point was at hand; the time had come for the public apology in three languages. Yet the audience still did not understand the meaning of what was about to occur and Kolasinski was determined not to enlighten them. He leaned forward, grasping the papers with both hands; his lips moved, but no sound was audible beyond several feet. Though his words a moment before had carried throughout the church, he now spoke barely above a whisper as he read the document Sbaretti and Foley had prepared.

I, Dominic Kolasinski, anxious to be reconciled with the church, to make my submission to the right reverend bishop of this diocese, do hereby make this my solemn retraction of all errors, and satisfaction for the evils and disorders which may justly be laid to my charge. I humbly ask pardon of God and His Church, of the Bishop and the people of this diocese, for all the scandal I have given during the last five years of disobedience to my lawful superiors, and by the exercise of priestly functions against the will and rightful authority of the right reverend bishop. I protest before God and before this congregation and all the people, that I am truly and sincerely sorry for all I have done contrary to the laws of God and the cannons of the Holy Church. I retract whatsoever I have said or done in opposition to the authority and jurisdiction of the right reverend bishop of this diocese. I will labor to promote peace and harmony between the people of this parish and their chief pastor, the right reverend bishop.

I pray God and His representative, the bishop, to accept this my humble reparation and submission; and I beg of God through the intercession of the most sweet heart of Mary, the grace to keep these promises for the honor of God and the good of souls. Amen.

First he read the statement in Polish, then quickly in German, and finally in English.

Those who may have expected him to beat his breast and raise his voice in public repentance were understandably annoyed. But the agreement with Sbaretti had said nothing of whether the apology was to be delivered fortissimo or pianissimo! (Orton, 1981: 142)

Father Kolasinski managed to maintain his stature in the Polish community and give many more years of service at Sweetest Heart of Mary Parish following his reconciliation.

The unifying of the whole Polish Catholic community under the jurisdiction of the Diocese of Detroit concludes this portion of the "Kolasinski Affair."

Reverend Francis A. Mueller

The Tenth Pastor of St. Albertus Parish

The tenth pastor of St. Albertus parish was Reverend Francis A. Mueller, whose mother was Polish. His long tenure and the role he played in guiding the founders of St. Mary of Czestochwa are significant to this research. After serving at St. Albertus for nineteen years, at forty-five Father Mueller died at his post, the only pastor to date to do so.

Father Mueller regarded himself as belonging to the Polish nationality and identified with the history, customs and religious traditions of his mother. He was loved by his parishioners, was eloquent in his Polish sermons and sensitively humane in his dealings. His American training and experience welded the parishioners into Polish-American Catholics.

Father Mueller's father died when he was only ten years old, but his widowed mother managed to send him to high school in Wroclaw, Poland. This may account for his Polish leanings. In 1885, Francis and his mother migrated to America. After being one of the first graduates from the Polish seminary started by Reverend Dabrowski (Father Kolasinski's adversary) in Detroit, Father Mueller completed his studies at St. Mary's Seminary in Baltimore. "

He was ordained by Bishop Foley October 4, 1891 in his home parish of St. Albertus in Detroit." (Swastek, 1973: 108) Following his ordination, Father Mueller was an assistant at St. Albertus for six months, then later returned to St. Albertus in 1894 after a two year assistant pastorate at Sacred Heart, a German Church in Detroit.

Father Francis Mueller brought a cooperative spirit and an ability to inspire and involve the congregation. Under his pastoral care St. Albertus paid off debts and prospered financially, while spiritual and ethnic needs were met through cherished traditions and fostering the heritage of piety and fortitude, of the Polish founding fathers. (Swastek, 1973: 1106-123)

Service of Tradition at St. Albertus in Detroit

Following the Second Vatican Council through the Archdiocesan Synod 69, ethnicity has been fostered, replenished and renewed at St. Albertus Parish in Detroit. The present pastor, (As of the writing of this research paper, 1982) Father Matlenga, is American born, of Polish descent and has been pastor since 1966. He developed four aspects of renewal in keeping with the directives of Vatican II. The third project applies directly to ethnicity. (Swastek, 1973: 172-175)

> Perhaps the most ambitious and spectacular project of Fr. Matlenga's renewal program inspired by Vatican II and Synod 69 was the Service of Tradition. The General Council spoke in several of its documents, but most notably in the Constitution of Divine Revelation, about tradition – its content, its importance, and the reverence due it. But the Council was speaking here of tradition in relation to the written Scriptures.
>
> In its Decree on the Missionary Activity of the Church, the Council spoke of tradition in another sense - as the complex of local native

"customs, outlook on life and social order (which) can be reconciled with the manner of living taught by divine revelation." The Council approved such particular traditions of particular churches which both reflected the genius and the dispositions of each nation and were accommodated to Christian Life.

Building on this notion of tradition, Fr. Matlenga gave his blessing to the enthusiastic zeal of several younger members of St. Albertus parish – notably Lawrence Chominski of the Liturgical Committee and Michael Krolewski of the Youth Club – who launched a concerted effort to revive the celebration of church feasts in the old traditional Polish Catholic style and manner. Once common in every Polish parish in Detroit and now observed occasionally in some, the traditional services had drawn capacity crowds in former decades. The youthful sponsors of the renewal, supported by Fr. Szopinski and approved by Fr. Matlenga, believed that these time-honored rites would still draw crowds of worshippers and make St. Albertus Church the cynosure of Polish eyes in Detroit.

Perhaps the most successful of these Services of Tradition was the Corpus Christi Procession held June 4, 1972, which drew an estimated crowd of 5,000 worshipers. ...

Among the participants in the colorful procession were young Polish Americans dressed in Polish regional folk costumes, several choirs, an orchestra, and representatives of numerous Polish societies. They had not seen such a religious celebration in decades. It drew tears of joy from the older worshipers, as they recalled the days of their youth. The young participants, on the other hand, sang with obvious joy and full-hearted enjoyment.

The Corpus Christi Procession was the second of its kind sponsored by the young people and by the societies of St. Albertus Parish. Its success was not the result of novelty appeal or effective publicity. The youthful advocates of the Service of Tradition had been at work for nearly two years, preparing traditional Polish celebrations. On two occasions, their petition for an old-fashioned Pasterka (Shepherd's Midnight Mass) brought nearly 2,000 worshipers from neighboring parishes and suburbs. ...

Polish saints also received recognition and veneration during the Service of Tradition. ...

Under youthful enthusiasm, the Service of Tradition is slowly but steadily expanding its horizons and activities. Most recently, a Polish country wedding ceremony was celebrated in St. Albertus Church, perhaps the first time such a rite was held in Detroit.

The Service of Tradition, more than any other parish activity, helped to make Detroiters, particularly those of Polish ancestry, aware of the approaching centenary of St. Albertus Parish. It also helped bring to the minds of older members of the congregation, who moved to the suburbs with their children or grandchildren, the memory of the golden days of old St. Albertus Parish, when it was the

Polish parish in the Detroit Diocese. It
reminded them of St. Albertus' past religious
and cultural leadership and perhaps – just
perhaps – made them hope that, if Polish
religious traditions and the Polish style of
Catholicism were to survive for future Detroit
generations to enjoy and cherish, the St.
Albertus Church might be the most fitting place
for such a shrine. (Swastek, 1973: 175-177)

While the previous quotation is lengthy, it is quoted verbatim, because it captures the spirit and enthusiasm of the "youthful" participants in planning and carrying on the Polish heritage of St. Albertus under the auspices of Services of Tradition. Obviously ethnicity is alive and well and thriving at St. Albertus Parish in Detroit, among the second, third, and even fourth generation Polonian Parishioners. With the present membership hovering around 500, there appears to be a hunger for expression of ethnicity among many more Americans born of Polish descent, when throngs ranging from 2,000 to 5,000 are attending traditional Polish services, at St. Albertus Church.

Theory Relationships

The most likely reasons for the establishment of St. Albertus were the numerical increase of Polish immigrants to the Detroit Areas, their desire to be ministered in their Polish language, and to engage in traditional Polish religious events. These founding members were opting for cultural pluralism, and frequently misread efforts at Americanization by Bishop Borgess as discrimination or hatred of Poles because of his German background.

There was much confusion over the English translation of St. Albertus. Why was an English translation of a Polish Saint necessary for a Polish Church title? Why did Father Simon find it important to register the baptisms and marriages in Latin and English, rather than Latin and Polish? This could be an assumption that the church was to play an Americanizing role.

Reverend Theodore Gieryk, a force for Cultural Pluralism, recognized the need to unify Polish people in the United States as one means of retaining their cultural traditions. He pointedly remarked that the partitioning powers in Poland had created artificial differences among Poles in America. By bringing to Detroit a newspaper, The Polish Catholic Gazette, he bolstered the Polish Catholic traditions in the community.

Father Dominek Kolasinski was Polish first and Catholic second. His appeal to the parishioners at St. Albertus was misunderstood by the hierarchy. He knew his people, their love of cultural traditions and their unquestioning loyalty to the Polish Catholic manner of following their religious convictions. He fulfilled their basic ethnic needs thus endearing himself to the members. The parishioners saw Reverend Josef Dabrowski as a rival of Father Kolasinski, therefore against them, for Kolasinski personified "Polishness" to his followers.

At various moments throughout the Kolasinski crises the newspapers both Polish and English were powerful forces for Americanization. The Polish people did not want to be identified as different from "Mainstream America," for this reduced their chances of moving up socially and economically. The insensitivity of Bishop Borgess toward the deep need for celebrating Midnight Mass in the traditional "Pasterka" manner deprived the parishioners of this ethnic expression of faith. Had he allowed the parishioners entrance to Mass at a neighboring parish, the historical crises may never have occurred and the chasm between him and his flock would have been easier to bridge.

Bishop Foley came nearest to being a force for the "Triple Melting Pot" with his emphasis on Catholicity at the expense of ethnicity, driving many Polish members from St. Albertus to the maverick church, Sweetest Heart of Mary.

Reverend Francis Mueller was at alternate times both a force for Cultural Pluralism and the "Triple Melting Pot." His fluency in Polish and identification with Polish history, customs and religious traditions fostered ethnicity during his parish term. He was, however, American trained at St. Mary's Seminary in Baltimore, ordained by Bishop Foley, and very much open to the idea of an emerging "American Catholic."

> Many Poles opted for the Melting Pot and all it represented, particularly the uniformity of suburbia as opposed to the uniqueness of Poletown. Many even changed their names.
>
> "They were under the false impression," said Father Matlenga, "that they would be more quickly advanced. Some of them working at Ford or the old car ship figured they'd get better jobs or better pay." (Trbovich, March 25, 1973)

Not all of the Polish people left St. Albertus because they were being assimilated into the community. In 1981 within a few blocks of St. Albertus a freeway cuts through Poletown.

Other homes and the Church of the Immaculate Conception are being razed to make way for another automobile plant, General Motors Corporation.

The attachment of the Polish-Americans to their parish and homes is being ignored in the name of progress. Some of the younger people were marrying and moving out of the area simply because housing was scarce.

Then integration pressure was being put on the Polish-Americans to whom the parish is considered family, and they wished to protect from intrusion.

The blacks moving into the neighborhood were not welcomed because they were not "Family." A group of parishioners banded together to support a senior citizens retirement center in their neighborhood hoping to replace the homes that were being demolished, with a safe place close to St. Albertus. No Poles were admitted to the project. They were told that the one hundred applications were lost. Eventually, the housing unit for the elderly housed all blacks.

The Poles had no choice but to move elsewhere. Today at St. Albertus Church and in the community surrounding the parish, Hispanic and Blacks are in greater numbers than the Poles.

"Not all moved because of enmity toward the blacks. Mrs. Pisarski, who moved to Sterling Heights (a suburb of Detroit), still returns to visit Emma McKinney, her black neighbor during her years in Poletown." (Trbovich, March 25, 1973)

Mrs. McKinney recognized the pride in home ownership and dedication to the Catholic Church of the Polish-Americans that lived in her neighborhood. Mrs. McKinney told The Free Press, newspaper reporter Marco Trbovich:

> We don't have that much trouble with the neighborhood, it's just that they (the newer residents) aren't as nice as them Polak people that moved out.
>
> ... or my belief and for what I know, I wouldn't live in a neighborhood without them Polish people. (March 25, 1973)

In spite of the rising crime rate in Detroit the present Polish-American parishioners of St. Albertus want to stay but many others are moving away for that reason.

The parishioners of St. Albertus rejected the Melting-Pot theory of socialization for Polish immigrants.

> The people accepted Americanization but at their own pace and in their own fashion, along the lines of biculturalism and bilingualism, admitting it into the school curriculums from the beginning and only much later into Church services. Aside from the Kolasinski Crisis, their attitudes toward and relations with local bishops were respectful and cooperative, but they expected a similar response from the bishops in matters touching on their traditional customs and practices. (Swastek, 1973: 196)

Is the role of St. Albertus declining or was the early definition of its role too narrow? The history of St. Albertus reveals "... the story of faith and courage – of kindly, humble, dignified people with idealism and integrity and pride in their Catholicism and their Polishness." (Swastek, 1973:197)

They left a legacy for future generations to cherish amid the social and economic changes including urban decay. "They demonstrated in a material way that a parish fostering the Polish style of Catholicism could be sustained in the free cosmopolitan climate of Detroit." (Swastek, 1973: 197)

Through its Service of Tradition the younger members of St. Albertus hope to preserve for future generations the traditions, services, and culture so dear to the early Polish Detroiters. St. Albertus is ...

... no mere reminder of a pioneer past peopled
with stouthearted men and women of
conviction and courage. St. Albertus Church is
today an exciting religious workshop for the
colorful ceremonies that are part of the Polish
style of Catholicism, reflecting not only its
distinctive spiritual qualities but also its vivid
folkloristic features. (Swastek, 1973: 198)

Soon after its centennial celebration St. Albertus Church was
designated a National Historic Site. At least the building will be
preserved from physical destruction, but a beautiful church with the
artifacts, statuary and memories, is a cold tribute to Polish-
Americans. The present parishioners desire a vital, full, dynamic
style of life for their Family of God at St. Albertus, Detroit, Michigan
while cherishing Polish-Catholic traditions.

4. St. Mary of Czestochowa in Dwight Township A State Historic Site

St. Mary of Czestochowa Parish serving 170 families is in a rural agricultural area. The church building is a small but stately red-brick structure with its interior measuring 5o by 100 feet. The statues and paintings have been appraised at over $100,000. its exterior size belies the enormous intensity of devotion of the Polish-American parishioners.

Even its history fills a mere two pages. The now deceased former pastor of St. Mary's, Rev. Henry S. Podsiad sketched a brief narrative of the development of the parish between the years of 1902 and 1948, quoted in its entirety below.

History of St. Mary's Parish

History of St. Mary's Parish originated in the year of 1902. Due to the lack of Polish speaking priest in St. Michael's Parish Port Austin, Michigan, and a long distance to travel through the woods, the first pioneers of Polish descent formed a committee and submitted a request to the Most Rt. Rev. Bishop John Foley of Detroit for permission to built a church. The permission was granted to the committee.

The committee consisted of the following men: Frank Koralewski, Jacob Polega, Stanislaus Koralewski, John Wojiechowski and George Zagorski. Frank Koralewski deeded 5 acres of land from his farm for the church site in Dwight Township, at that present time the town of Kinde was not in existance.

The people themselves builded the church, a frame building with the capacity of 200. They did not have the money to pay for the material, so Stanley Koralewski mortgaged his farm in order to get the money to pay for the material.

The church was noted the St. Mary of Czestochowa. After the church was completed the Most Rev. Bishop John Foley sent the first Pastor, the Rev. Julian Trzetrzynski on October 6, 1903 and was a pastor to December 10, 1905. The next pastor was the Rev. John B. Hewelt from 1905 to September 23, 1910. During his pastorate there were about 70 families. The parish embraced Kinde and Rapson.

The Rev. Boleslaus Stefanski became Pastor on September 23, 1910 to January 9, 1922 during his pastorate the people from Kinde left St. Mary's Church and built their own church in the town of Kinde.

St. Joseph's church in Rapson, Michigan was a mission to the St. Mary's Church during the Rev. Father Stefanski's pastorage.

The Rev. Raphael Chrzaszcz was appointed the next pastor from January 1922 to January 15, 1924. During that time Fr. Chrzaszcz also took charge of St. Joseph Mission in Rapson.

The Rev. Xavier Rosinski was appointed pastor January1924 to October 1925. In 1925 the St. Joseph's Mission in Rapson became a parish, and their own pastor the Rev. Father Sajnaj.

In October 1925 The Rev. Alexander Szumowski was appointed a Pastor to June 15, 1929.

On June 15, 1929 the Rev. Harry S. Podsiad succeeded the Rev. Father Szumowski as Pastor and found 60 families. At the end of the year of 1929 the debts were paid off to the bank and to Mr. Stanley Koralewski who mortgaged his farm to upkeep the St. Mary's Church. At that present time he was also the organist of the parish. The buildings were in all good condition.

In the year of 1932, May 29, on Corpus Christi Day a fire broke out and destroyed the church to the ground. The same year a new church was built of cobble stones, and brick, the capacity of 504.

During the construction of the building the parishioners volunteered their time and work. The cost of the new church completed was $15,000.00. The corner stone was laid on the 3rd day of September 1932, by the Most Rt. Rev. Bishop Joseph Plagens Auxiliary Bishop of Detroit. The dedication of the new church took place on May 28, 1933. The Most Rt. Rev. Bishop Michael Gallagher officiated.

On October 10, 1933 the barn and garage burned. During the months of November and December a new garage was built with the help of the parishioners at the cost $600.00.

In the year of 1937 the church was decorated, the cost of $1,200.00.

Water proofing of the church was being done from the steeple to the foundation, also copper installation in the year of 1946, at the cost $6,500.00.

Marble was installed in the church with the help of the parishioners in the year of 1947, the cost of $4,000.00. Also the windows were reinstated and storm windows put in at the cost of $2,200.00.

The decoration of the church and new fixtures were installed the same year for $6,000.00.

Asphalt was laid with the help of the parishioners at the cost of $2,000.00. Tile was laid in the year of 1948.

At present there are 98 families. The parish is free of debts.

The services are conducted in Polish and English languages.

Rev. Henry S. Podsiad – Pastor

What may appear as misspelling or typographical errors in the quotation may be attributed to the Polish priest not being fully educated in the English language.

Rev. Podsiad retired June 15, 1967 after 38 years of service.

The determined Polish-Americans desired to expand their thriving parish to fulfill more needs of the community. They purchased land in 1953, west of the church rectory. In 1954 the present auditorium was completed there and dedicated. The cemetery is on the east side of the church building in which a lighted "Crucifix group" was installed in 1958. One year later a new garage was added.

In 1960 an artist was commissioned to paint the murals that adorn the ceiling of the church building. The name of the artist is unknown. In his humility he refused to sign his work. In three different articles the ancestry of the artist is said to be Polish, Indian, and in the third, Italian. But the last is most certainly confusing the paintings with the Shrine to Our Lady of Czestochowa which was made and imported from Rome. More frequently Polish and Native American Indian are indicated, but whispered rumor is that it was a Polish/Indian of mixed ancestry. We will never know for sure because Polish is the dominant cultural background of the area so his Polishness would be important to the people. The murals depict incidents in the life of Jesus and Mary. Painted on canvas the murals were then sealed in a type of plastic and affixed to the ceiling.

Between the church structure and the auditorium is the Shrine to Our Lady of Czestochowa, Michigan's only shrine to Poland's patron saint. Patricia Mroczek interviewed Chester A. Kozdroj for the newspaper, The Huron Daily Tribune. Kozdroj elaborated on the historical background for the original painting of Our Lady of Czestochowa, lovingly referred to as "The Black Madonna."

Kozdroj studied at the University of Krakow and University of Warsaw, both in Poland, and also taught for a number of years at St. Mary's College at Orchard Lake. He and Monsignor Vincent Borkowicz are the two oldest members of the Board of Regents at Orchard Lake, having served about four decades.

According to the tradition, Kozdroj said, the portrait of Our Lady of Czestochowa was painted by St. Lucas the Evangelist during the lifetime of the Blessed Virgin Mary. It was painted on a tabletop used by the Holy Family, the legend says.

In the fourth century, St. Helen, the mother of Emperor Constantine The Great, brought the portrait to Constantinople, Turkey.

In the ninth or tenth century, the painting reached the lands of Poland and was placed at Belzkin castle, on the northeast side of Lwow, known as Rus Czrwona.

In 1382, Prince Wladyslaw of Opola (who in the name of King Ludwik of Hungry) moved the painting from the Belzkin castle in order to protect it from the numerous pagan attacks of Tatars and Turks. The decision to move the sacred portrait came after a besieging of the castle. A Tatar arrow shot through the window of the chapel and allegedly struck the neck of Our Lady, Kozdroj said.

Prince Wladslaw decided to take the painting to Opla in Slask for safeguarding, Kozdroj explained.

During the trip, the travelers stopped to rest near Czestochowa.

"Tradition says Our Lady appeared to the Prince and told him she wanted to remain there," Kozdroj said.

The prince took the portrait to Jasna Gora, a high hill overlooking the town of Czestochowa. It was left under the protection of white Pauline Fathers brought from Hungary, according to the tradition.

August 26, 1382 was named as the final resting date in history for the Painting of Our Lady of Czestochowa, Kozdroj said.

Kozdroj said the oldest mention of this holy painting was found in first written history of Poland. It was written by Jan Dlugosz in "Lbr Beneficiorum," about 70 or 80 years after the final resting place of the fame portrait at Czestochowa. Dlugosz lived near Czestochowa and is credited as having authored an accurate account. Kozdroj said.

Miraculous events throughout history are attributed to the painting and pious prayers before Our Lady, Kozdroj said. He particularly sited a battle at the city of Vienna during which Polish King Jan Sobieski conquered the Turks and permanently stopped the besieging of Europe.

"Poland and Europe were being invaded by Turks. The last stand was at the city of Vienna ... who begged our Polish King to help. He mobilized his army ... prayed to Our Lady ... and marched against the Turks."

Kozdroj said the Polish King proclaimed to the Turks, "... that he is the Savior of Europe." He sent the Pope a communication that said, "In the name of the Blessed Mother, please let me help defeat the Turks," Kozdroj said.

History tells that the Blessed Mother interceded in the battle and that of the 25,000 knights who died, only 1,000 of them were Polish, he added.

To the Pope another memo was sent, Kozdroj that it stated: "I came, I saw, God Conquered."

Kozdroj said he has visited the sacred shrine at Czestochowa and seen great treasures on a giant altar that have been left by grateful people who received favors from Our Lady.

At Czestochowa, there is now a facsimile over the original portrait. Kozdroj said a solemn ceremony is observed during huge pilgrimages that attract hundreds of thousands of people. During the ceremony, trumpets blast and the facsimile is electrically raised to expose the Black Madonna.

"It is totally humbling," Kozdroj said. "In fact, we have never seen such piety, such devotion. It moves you ... the piety." "We were crying," he added.

The Struggle for Ethnic Survival Begins

In St. Mary of Czestochowa Parish in Kinde in Dwight Township in Michigan, the story of ethnic retention has not been gratifying. There ethnicity was threatened by suppression from the now retired Bishop Reh of the Saginaw Diocese. This issue is misunderstood in America even today. The local newspapers implied by their coverage, that the case at Dwight Township was another problem of "Trusteeism," in which the parishioners desire control of the property, wealth, and administration of church affairs. (Nuesse and Harte, 1950: 47)

In the minutes of St Mary of Czestochowa Parish Council for March 25, 1980 was the simple notation:

> A committee from both St. Mary's and St Edwards will meet Friday 11:00 am with Bishop Reh to try to keep both parishes open. From St. Mary, Ron Yaroch, alternate Mary Rice. We are also trying to keep the name St. Mary of Czestochowa as is, even if the churches are amalgamated.

The meeting was the beginning of a confrontation that was to get more heated as the months passed even with Bishop Reh threatening excommunication to all the parishioners. Unlike the controversy at Saint Albertus, the priests at Dwight Township managed to keep a low profile except for a change of parish at the request of Rev. Ronald Dombrowski who was at St. Mary's of Czestochowa early in the proposed merger.

A meeting on March 28, 1980 was called to discuss the pros and cons of the suppression of the two parishes. Prior to this meeting a survey was taken at both churches. St. Edwards is a territorial parish and the members there supported the status quo. St. Mary of Czestochowa, a Juridical National Parish, had the most to lose, including its name, statuary, and the ceiling murals. The minutes of the meeting at the Diocesan Chancery Office reflect the adamant stand of Bishop Reh to "canonically suppress" the two parishes of St. Mary of Czestochowa and St. Edward. What he did not anticipate were the deeply rooted ethnic parishioners' commitment to their Polish-American Catholicism.

The tone of the meeting was set with the answers of Bishop Reh to the first two questions.

> The question was asked if both churches could be kept open?
>
> Bishop Reh said in Kinde, a new parish would be formed with one community entailing the canonical supresion (sic.) of both present benefices. The situation to be similar to Sebwaing-Unionville, with the exception that the building and sites of both parishes would be utilized for the one new parish.
>
> Will St. Mary's still remain an ethnic parish?
>
> Bishop: No.

The St. Mary's parish representatives could see no real changes in facilities or priestly services. Since 1974 both parishes had been served by one priest and the buildings of both had been utilized. The main changes proposed were the renaming of the parishes under one title and the suppression of the Polish language, liturgies, and traditions at St. Mary of Czestochowa.   One concession Bishop Reh made was that the Shrine of Our Lady of Czestochowa could remain intact.

Later in the meeting the question was asked, "Why the hurry in making this change?" Bishop Reh responded with, "Time will not serve a good purpose." It was time that eventually saved St. Mary of Czestochowa from suppression, time for appeals, court action, and a new ethnically sensitive bishop.

After hearing about the intent of the Bishop to liquidate their parish, the existing parish council contacted Harry Milostan, attorney, counselor, and author to act on their behalf and to guide them in their fight to keep their church, and the name of St. Mary of Czestochowa and "to retain their Polish heritage and culture." He composed a letter. Basically it asks many questions but nowhere does it suggest that the membership wants to control the property or wealth, only to have a say in retention of ethnicity. Bishop Reh represents an attempt to destroy ethnicity and ignores the traditional role of its legal existence.

The role of Henry Milostan was to enlarge until the culmination of the crisis, almost a year after the initial meeting with Bishop Reh by the committee from St. Mary's.

The Saginaw Diocesan office verbally denied that St. Mary of Czestochowa was a "National" parish therefore had no more rights than any other territorial parish. Ralph Majewski then telephoned the Archdiocese of Detroit under which St. Mary's had been established. The Archivist Leonard P. Blair responded by letter with:

> My search through our archives only confirmed what I told you then; namely, that if any original papers did exist, they would have been forwarded to Saginaw when that diocese was first established. We have no such papers here.

Grandchildren of the founding parishioners finally located copies or the original deed to the land stating that it was to be used for a "Polish Catholic Church to be named St. Mary of Czestochowa in honor of the Patron of Poland." Upon finding a "Parish Survey" dated April 26, 1940 by Pastor, Rev. Podsiad and September 25, 1941 by a "Visitator," Guillelmus from the Saginaw Chancery, the parishioners had substantial proof that their parish was both historically and officially designated a Polish "National" parish under the protection of the Holy See.

The Parish Council of St. Mary of Czestochowa then turned to Pope John Paul II hoping that his Polish background would favor their cause. Three of the five facts in this letter refer to retention of ethnicity. These desperate people ask for: "Pastoral care in the Polish language," "to retain (their) identity and the name of (their) church," and from the Holy Father, "a stay of execution."

One can imagine the frustration the members of St. Mary of Czestochowa felt when trying to plead their case to someone who would listen and possibly influence Bishop Reh to reconsider the closing of their beloved church building. Mr. Deward Korolewski in his attempt to reach Cardinal Wyszynski received this reply.

> Dr. Mr. Korolewski:
>
> This will inform you that your letter of June 8, 1980 addressed to Cardinal Wyszysnski, has been referred back, as the custom is, to this office.
>
> Very truly yours,
>
> Msgr. Eugene A. Frobes
>
> Vicar General

Monsignor Eugene A. Forbes was the recording secretary at the March 28, 1980 meeting with Bishop Reh, therefore, Mr. Deward Korolewski's letter ended up in the Saginaw Chancery Office.

Indicative of Bishop Reh's point of view is the following response to a concerned member of St. Mary of Czestochowa parish.

> I find it hard, however, to understand your insistence on a National Polish Parish. The whole trend in this country and from Rome is rather that parishes should be open to everybody and not to just nationals. National parishes were set up in the United States for immigrants. I am sure you do not consider the good people of St. Mary of Czestochowa as still being immigrants in the United States. I am quite surprised that you are insisting about service to Polish people because as far as I know, a very large number of Polish families

are parishioners of St. Edward Parish. I understand that sometimes there can be a brother in one parish and a sister in another. Are we Christians or are we Polish?

... Please let's be Christians and not Polish or German (as I am) or Slovak or Irish or anything else. St. Paul taught that there was to be no distinction between Jew or Greek (all the same Lord). And now you write me that you want to stay a National Polish Parish. I am surprised at you. ...

St. Mary of Czestochowa "was always open to everyone and services were always in both the English and Polish Languages" (letter to Pope). In an interview with Ralph Majeski, he explained that at this time (September 28, 1980) there is no Polish priest, therefore no Polish Mass or services, but prior to this problem there was only one Mass in Polish and two Masses in English and frequently St. Edward parishioners attended services. In the summer "pilgrims" from all over Michigan come to celebrate Mass.

Since Harry Milostan, the attorney engaged for advice, received no reply to his letter to Bishop Reh he composed another letter to be sent to the media to awaken an awareness among Polish-Americans of the problems facing St. Mary of Czestochowa parishioners.

An Ardent Plea to the Pope

Bishop Reh ordered the disbanding of both the Parish Councils of St. Edward and St. Mary of Czestochowa so that a joint council could be established for the newly organized parish. On August 8, 1980 the parishioners of St. Mary of Czestochowa set up a Parish Committee to continue to battle with Bishop Reh. A more extensive letter was drafted for presentation to Pope John Paul II by third generation Polonians, because Bishop Reh had set the date of closing for September 13, 1980. Again the main complaint "... Bishop Reh appears completely unaware of the value and importance of a rooted culture and inheritance of nationality to cherish and strengthen the religious life." Two official acknowledgements from the Vatican that both letters had been received are in the hands of parishioners. The following letter is a translation of the Polish letter addressed to Pope John Paul II from the Parish Committee of St. Mary of Czestochowa.

His Holiness Pope John Paul II   August 8, 1980

Vatican – Rome – Italy

Dearest, Our Pride, Holy Father!

We, the third generation of the original founders and donors of the Parish of St. Mary of Czestochowa, which is threatened with closing, are turning to you, the Father of all the world's faithful, with an ardent plea to assist us in saving our Polish, ethnic parish of St. Mary of Czestochowa in Kinde, the diocese of Saginaw, state of Michigan, where to the time of his resignation, the ordinary was Bishop Francis Reh.

We are, poor and diminished in spirit, parishioners, ordinary farmers, and home owners, descendents of Polish pioneers, who in the year 1903 established and with their own blacksmithing 77 years ago, laid the foundation stone and began building a church under the name of St. Mary of Czestochowa, and which church, under the decree of Bishop Reh, has been ordered liquidated.

We were startled by this decision of Bishop Reh to merge our Polish Parish with a nearby territorial parish of St. Edward which was established in 1917, and in its place found a new territorial church under a new name. This parish would use the church of St. Mary of Czestochowa, which would be stripped of all memorials, paintings, statues, stained windows and any signs of ethnicity in order not to offend, eventually, some of the newly joining (against their will) parishioners of St. Edwards.

Bishop Re, whose retirement has already been approved by Your Holiness, is hurrying this liquidation before his leave-taking, and we understand, is also attempting the same action in other Polish parishes of the diocese of Saginaw. This diocese is comprised of a large percentage of Americans of Polish descent, especially farmers who have retained very strong feelings of their heritage and have inherited Polish roots of deep religious devotion, love of customs, and traditions and an attachment to the Church and its ethnicity.

In contrast to his predecessors, Bishop Stephen Woznicki and the newly-appointed present Archbishop of Washington, D. C., Bishop James Hickey, Bishop Reh appears completely unaware of the value and importance of a rooted culture and inheritance of nationality to cherish and strengthen the religious life. With an eagerness and zeal, worthy of more important matters, together with his commissions and advisors, he began the liquidation of Polish parishes against the wishes and needs of the good-hearted Polish people.

Regretfully we have become aware that he has not attempted to secure pastors who would have been able to do pastoral work in both languages. For the last several years, we parishioners have been deprived of Mass, devotions and sacraments in the Polish language. Some of them yearned painfully for Polish Confessions, as well as homilies and songs at the funerals of our parents and relatives. The retiring Bishop mistakenly, it seems to us, interprets the documents of the Second Vatican Council.

Because the final closing of the parish of St. Mary of Czestochowa by decree of Bishop Reh will occur on the 13th of September, and since our pleas to Bishop Reh have received no hearing, it is in Your Holy Father that we have our only hope and assistance. We beg you, Dear Father of all the faithful of the world, help us, ordinary people, farmers, widows, descendants of Your faithful sons and sons of the Blessed Mother of Czestochowa; help us for we shall be lost.

Faithful to You, Traditions, and the Faith of Our Fathers,

The Parish Committee of St. Mary of Czestochowa (Signed by the Committee Members)

Desperate Committee Turns to Civil Courts

Since no decision had arrived from Rome, in desperation the committee looked to the State of Michigan for a stay of "execution." Two lines of defense were used. A petition was filed with the Michigan History Division, Historic Sites Research Unit on October 16, 1980.

> 20.   HISTORICAL SIGNIFICANCE:
>
> Under Prussian domination in the 1840's very religious Roman Catholic Polish people departed their beloved homeland for America. Many to Huron and Sanilac Counties in Michigan. St. Michael Parish in Port Austin, established in 1868, was attended by Polish immigrants who finally, after recognizing the need to retain their national ethnic values, moved in 1902 to establish St. Mary of Czestochowa Parish in their own community of Dwight Township. The parish name has significance in that Our Lady (St. Mary) of Czestochowa is the Patron Saint of Poland.

This is the first known Roman Catholic parish in Michigan to be so named. (From a copy of the original petition)

The second course of action took the Committee through Attorney H. Dale Cubitt of Bad Axe, Michigan, to the courts. After they filled nineteen complaints the plaintiffs asked:

Wherefore, plaintiffs pray that the defendant (Bishop Reh) be ordered:

A. To show cause why a preliminary injunction should not be issued enjoining him and his agents from:

1. Terminating the national parish status of St. Mary of Czestochowa,

2. Amalgamating said parish with the Parish of St. Edward's,

3. Closing or ceasing to use St. Mary of Czestochowa for normal church functions,

4. Renovating St. Mary of Czestochowa by removing or moving the altars, the ceiling and wall paintings and statues and other art objects without the advice and/or consent of the parish council.

B. That a temporary restraining order be granted without notice or hearing until a hearing can be held in the above entitled matter; (From a copy of the document filed in the Circuit Court for the County of Huron).

The complaint was filed on August 19, 1980 and the restraining order issued the same day.

In response to this action Bishop Reh sent a letter to the Parishes of St. Mary of Czestochowa and St. Edward. A reprint was available from The Citizen, a newspaper in Hamtramck, which was covering the struggles at St. Mary of Czestochowa from almost the beginning in its column, The History of Detroit's Polonia by Lawrence Chominski.

> ... Anyone may have recourse to our Holy Father, the Pope, I could never object to that. I even told some of you to present the matter to him if you wished. I would welcome that he have the whole story.
>
> But instead, some have dared to have their Bishop summoned publicly to the civil court. If the case is presented to Rome, I hope the Holy Father will never learn of this! It would give him pain. I am afraid he, too, would be ashamed that some Catholics, Polish too, violated the canon law of the Church, which is his law as Pope, to bring his brother-bishop before the civil court!
>
> I hope he never learns of it. Because it is the law of the Church that a bishop may not be summoned to a civil court without the express permission of the Holy See. Violation of this law is punished with immediate excommunication!
>
> I'm sure those who did this awful thing did not realize that it is a crime by church law; and so they could be considered as not having suffered the penalty of excommunication. But I do hope that our poor Holy Father never learns about this for his own sake and for your sake.

My dearly beloved, we are not to use our different cultures as something to keep us separated in the Church. We are all to contribute the benefits of our own culture to one another. This is what Catholics of many different origins have done in our country to make one beautiful enriched American Catholic Church. (1980: October 9)

There is the impression that Bishop Reh, as a prelate in the Catholic Church, would also know that it states in Canon Law: "... That no change be made with regard to national parishes without the approval of the Holy See." (Canon 216, No. 4) For whom did he not wish the Holy Father to hear of this situation, the Pope's sake? ... the parishioners? ... or could it have been Bishop Reh?

Why did bishop Reh persist in setting the date for the closing and removal of "Polishness" from St. Mary of Czestochowa, when he knew full well that a definitive reply from the Vatican had not yet arrived? It was his unrelenting pressures that drove the faithful from St. Mary of Czestochowa to appeal to the Civil Court. Not even the threat of excommunication, with the ultimate punishment of spending eternity in hell, could stop the membership from fighting to retain their Polish identity. The last paragraph in the quotation from Bishop Reh's letter implied that the Polish-Americans at Dwight have nothing in the Polish Catholic culture worth preserving.

In spite of all the objections of the parishioners, on September 3, 1980 Bishop Reh issued two Decrees. These were issued after the bishop had received and surprisingly accepted the restraining order from the Civil Court (Jajeski, 1980).

The First Decree:

Suppressing the Parish of St. Edward, Kinde
Michigan with its traditional boundaries, and the
Parish of St. Mary (Dwight), Kinde Michigan
with its traditional boundaries – which parishes
will be re-established into a new parish with
new boundaries by further decree.

The last paragraph on the first page of this decree lists the
parishes consulted. Neither St. Mary of Czestochowa nor St.
Edward's were involved. However, St. Michael's of Port Austin, the
very church from which the Polish founders of St. Mary's felt the
need to separate, was included. In the suppression decree was also
the revocation of "all rights and privileges, and obligations proper to
them as parishes of this Diocese of Saginaw."

The Second Decree:

Establishing the parish of St. Mary of the Virgin
and St. Edward the Confessor, Kinde, Michigan
with determined boundaries, to serve the needs
of the community of Kinde, Michigan.

... Divine worship in the new parish is to be
held immediately in the hall adjacent to the
Dwight Church in order that the liturgical
renovations called for by the Fathers of the
Second Vatican Council in its Constitution on
the Sacred Liturgy and by the directives of the
Liturgical Commission of the National Council
of Catholic Bishops may be accomplished
without delay.

Bishop Reh did not come to celebrate the last Mass at these churches as he had planned. In this second Decree, while mentioning the directive of the Liturgical Commission based on the liturgical renovations called for by the Fathers of the Second Vatican Council, he does not specifically mention any section of the Vatican II Documents. He apparently has some view of American Culture in order to comply with Part II, "Some Problems of Special Urgency," Chapter II, The Proper Development of Culture" but his perspective does not include a place for the Juridical National Parish in the Roman Catholic Church in the United States of America.

Historic Event for Our Lady

On August 24, 1980 hundreds of visitors overflowed St. Mary of Czestochowa Church, in a special Polish traditional celebration in honor of six hundred years of devotion to St. Mary of Czestochowa. Lawrence Chominski elaborated in The Citizen newspaper:

> Powerful moral support came from within the very ramparts of Polish Catholicism and tradition in Michigan's Orchard Lake (The Polish Seminary), the Polish parishes in Hamtramck and Detroit, the Polish American Congress (present membership 1.5 million), and other organizations. (September 4, 1980: 9)

Patricia Mroczek in The Huron Tribune newspaper covered the days festivities in pictures and words:

> Three priests and Monsignor Zdzislaw Peszkowski of St. Mary's Catholic Church, Orchard Lake, officiated at the ceremony for Our Lady of Czestochowa, the saint that is the "Holiest of Holy" of Poland.

St. Mary of Czestochowa Church hosted the sacred services in conjunction with its annual festival to draw attention to its fight toward the preservation of the church's Polish ethnicity. In March, the Saginaw Diocese announced that the church would be closed September 15, 1980, and merged with St. Edward's Catholic Church into a new territorial church for the Kinde area. (August 25, 1980)

Monsignor later received a reprimand from Bishop Reh for coming in from the Archdiocese of Detroit and causing interference.

Processions are a popular tradition among the Polish in the Catholic Church. It was natural that a beautiful, colorful procession began the ceremonies. Patricia Mroczek continues her coverage:

Her article is printed here in its entirety because it presents the deep seated appreciation of the Polish culture by the Polish people in the United States of America.

A blonde altar boy, clad in an all-white long gown and carrying a tall golden cross, began the services by leading the procession down the middle aisle of the parish.

Small children, carrying red and white gladiolas (the Polish colors) served as honor guards.

Ninety-one-year-old Mrs. Frank Lerash of Kinde, carried a portrait of Polish Pope John Paul II in the long processional line. The painting was blessed and will hang on display at the church, St. Mary of Czestochowa Church.

Four teenaged girls then carried a special processional display of white linen to accent the portrait of the Black Madonna (Our Lady of Czestochowa and her Child).

Concluding the marchers were Parish Administrator Rev. Francis J. Murray (who relieved Rev. Ron Dombrowski) former pastor Rev. Stanley Surman of St. Mary's Parisville, and former pastor Rev. Barney Janowicz of Holy Trinity, Bay City, who joined the monsignor.

As the procession began to move up the aisle, the organ played a prelude and the large congregation filled the church with the harmonious chorus of a Polish song.

Church member Ralph Majeski described the Polish choir interspersed in the crowd as "unbelievable."

"It made tears come to my eyes when the inside of our church filled with those Polish voices," Majeski said.

Peszkowski had credited Majeski with organizing the "historic event for our Lady."

Majeski explained why he and a small committee planned the ceremonious services:

"I did it for the sake of the people who believe in St. Mary's of Czestochowa church ... for all the years they've come.

"I did it for the older people ... and for the younger people so they can get a feeling of what it's all about and continue with the tradition of Our Lady,"

Majeski said the services gave him "goose-bumps ... it was so beautiful."

"It taught me to be proud of your name, because your name will be with you forever," he added.

Peszkowski gave the sermon during the Mass. He told the large, quiet crowd that, fourteen days ago, he was at Jasna Gora, the high hill where the historic Black Madonna is on display near Czestochowa, Poland. While in Poland, Peszkowski spoke with part of the 27,000 people who walked the nine days from Warsaw to Czestochowa to pray before Our Lady, he said. "I told those people about this parish and its fight to keep its identity." "When you are talking of Our Lady of Czestochowa, we are talking of our heritage," Peszkowski added.

"We must be strong," Peszkowski said, stirring the crowd. "Every third Pole is out of Poland."

The monsignor said Poland and its people must "fight all the time for our identity ... it is necessary to fight all the time for our name."

"I beg of you. Use your imagination ... for the most precious things we have are our immortal soul and our name."

A New Bishop

A New Hope - Revival of Polish Ethnicity

A young priest of German descent was appointed to replace Bishop Reh, but it was not until February of 1981 that the case of St. Mary of Czestochowa could be considered. A quiet meeting with the new Bishop Kenneth Untener together with concerned parishioners (including Ralph Majeski and a copy of an earlier study of the Juridical National Parish written by Jean Marie Miscisin) was held at a nearby Parish, St. Mary's of Parisville. Without much fanfare the new Bishop withdrew all procedures for the closing of the parishes of St. Edward and St. Mary of Czestochowa.

By March 1981 the newly assigned pastor Rev. Harry Sikorski, a Polish speaking priest was serving both parishes, St. Mary of Czestochowa with 95% Polish-American parishioners and St. Edward with at least 50% Polish-American parishioners. The year long struggle to retain their ethnicity had come to an end. To my knowledge Pope John Paul II because of more pressing matters had not yet replied to the urgent pleas, but now he will be notified of the satisfactory solution to the problems of St. Mary of Czestochowa Parish.

Theory Relationships

Harry Milostan recognized and name "Cultural Pluralism" as the sociological direction desired by parishioners of St. Mary's of Czestochowa and accepted by members of St. Edward's. Although removed socially and economically from the farming community, he understood and appreciated the position of the Polish-American Catholics in Dwight Township. His knowledge of the American legal system and his love of the Polish-Catholic traditions allowed him to serve a unique role in guiding the parishioners. Setting aside the American value of remuneration, allowed his "Polishness" to set his course of action.

Bishop Reh, the main force for "Americanization" frequently made references to Catholic or Christian first, or placed Polish and Catholic in juxtaposition. Only in the United States could Bishop Reh have been presented the problem of making the decision to suppress a Juridical National Parish. The need of these parishes does not exist in any other country, because the United States alone is a land of immigrants and their descendants. Bishop Reh believed in the monolithic nature of Catholicism yet diversity was rampant at the Second Vatican Council, thus causing the seemingly contradictory interpretation of its directives by American Bishops. Since all the directives could not be implemented at once, each bishop was free to begin placing emphasis at his discretion. Bishop Reh placed his emphasis on unity and the American way, which leans heavily on Anglo-Saxon traditions with Irish hierarchical predominance.

The parishioners of St. Mary's of Czestochowa received moral support from Polish-Americans throughout Michigan by newspaper coverage. Through the Polish-American Congress word of the fight to remain an ethnic parish spread to neighboring states. From this it is apparent that Cultural Pluralism is not an isolated phenomenon of large cities. This bond of the Polish-American persists even with social/economic mobility.

In the small rural parish of St. Mary of Czestochowa in Dwight Township the Polish-American Catholics are rejoicing at the assignment of a Polish priest as pastor. Mass homilies and hymns are now heard in Polish. Liturgies and celebrations again follow the Polish cultural traditions. For the ninety-five percent Polish-American congregation, St. Mary of Czestochowa again serves the original role for which it was established.

Unlike St. Albertus in Detroit, St. Mary of Czestochowa parish is in an agricultural area where modernization includes up-to-date tractors and produce production methods, where Americanization forces are minimal. Urbanization with the accompanying social and economic changes will not reach this parish in the foreseeable future. Freeways and industries do not disturb this community's cohesiveness.

There is a sense of gratitude among the Polish-Americans of the third, fourth, and fifth generation for the democratic form of self-government in the United States. To them the rights and privileges carry a corresponding responsibility to be good citizens and render unto the government the things that are the governments' and to God the things that are God's, but in uniquely Polish ways.

Young families build new homes on inherited property. If children do move away the old homestead remains as solid evidence of the roots set down by their forefathers who came to the United States and stayed because they loved their land, their homes, their freedom, their church, and their Polish heritage. All these values will be fostered at St. Mary of Czestochowa so that future generations may worship in the traditional Polish Catholic manner.

5. All Saints Roman Catholic Church

Flint, Michigan

All Saints Parish in the city of Flint did not have the problems of a legal or hierarchical nature. It was one of cooperation and respect between ethnic groups right from its establishment.

The story of the first 25 years at All Saints was briefly stated in a large Silver Jubilee book with the pages divided in half. The story in the Polish language appears on the left of the page and English translation on the right. I was told it was not verbatim, but the content was the same.

> On February 23, 1910, the Most Reverend Bishop John S. Foley, Bishop of Detroit, appointed Rev. Fr. Boleslaus Stafanski, then Assistant at St. Adalberts (again the old spelling of St. Albertus but upon checking the history of St. Albertus Fr. Stafanski was assistant there) Church in Detroit to be the first pastor of All Saints Parish in Flint, Michigan. The good heartedness of the late Fr. Murphy, Pastor of St. Michael Church (predominantly Irish Catholic Church) made it possible for the new pastor to gather the Poles for Mass in St. Michael Church.

Please note the use of the word Parish to designate the Polish people because there was no church building named All Saints when the priest was appointed.

Financial management of All Saints went smoothly even when there were major changes in specifications for the buildings. Only three weeks into construction Fr. Stafanski was transferred and Fr. John B. Hewlet came from Kinde in Huron County (St. Mary of Czestochowa, as St. Edward was not established until 1917) to serve in his place.

Under Father Hewlet's direction All Saints Parish grew, both in memberships and structures. A church, school, and magnificent rectory were built.

From the very early years All Saints Parish welcomed other peoples of all nationalities and backgrounds as stated in the Silver Jubilee History.

> McFarling and O'Connor and similar names form a whole group of the parishioners in the second year of All Saints Church, and further records at every letter, show a great change from the original exclusively Polish list to an international congregation. It is not exaggerated, to claim that in the second year of the Parish's existence over 500 families joined All Saints Parish.

Although there were no dramatic and complicated controversies in All Saints there were internal conflicts which appear to involve personalities and undocumented rumors. Quoting again from the Silver Jubilee History:

> With the great success of Father Hewlet's work there is a mysterious opposition arising in the parish. How it happened, where it came from, nobody seems to be in a condition to explain now and those that were mixed in the

reversals of the career of the dear Father---are silent. There are nevertheless, facts known to the senior public and noted by Father Hewelt himself, for instance: in 1914, the annual report shows a great decrease in the number of families belonging to the parish. From over 500 in 1911, in the 1914 remained less than 300. Who abandoned the parish and why---nobody knows.

"The 'Independents' have worked hard to get the separatist Poles, dissatisfied with Father Hewlet's administration and tactics, to join their new 'Non-Catholic' but 'Polish' churches on Michigan Avenue and on Selby Street, but their efforts were only temporarily successful. In 1917, when Father Hewlet's political importance grew, dissatisfaction also increased to such a point that in 1920, September 24th, the Most Reverend bishop Gallagher succeeded in inducing Father Hewelt to resign pastorate of All Saints Parish and accept a place in St. Joseph's Parish, Jackson, Michigan.

The opposition formed in Flint extended also to Jackson, where a simple refusal of the Parish to accept the appointment of Father Hewelt, caused his early retirement from public life.

On the same day, that is, September 24th, 1920, Bishop Gallagher appointed to the pastorate of All Saints Parish in Flint, the Reverend Fr. Athanasius F. Polanowski former Pastor of St. Joseph's Church in Jackson, Michigan.

All Saints Church Affiliation

The sections of the History of all Saints revealing the integrating forces and respect for all ethnic groups are the following two paragraphs on church membership and the description of the Jubilee Program.

How are parishioners affiliated with the Church? The old system prevailing in many parishes of Polish origin is the pew-rent. The latest system is the envelope set either for families or for individuals. The All Saints Parish uses both systems. There are about 600 pews rented, although just about 200 are actually paid. There are about 750 envelope sets distributed but actually only some few hundreds are using them regularly. House collections, fuel collections, and school records bring in names not included in the first two systems. The attendance on Sundays of services exceeds 3,000, but we cannot call everyone a parishioner. An accurate list of membership is therefore impossible. We figure in families a membership of 800 families, and in souls, about 5,000 souls---somehow connected with the Parish. It would be proper to divide this membership into three (3) groups, one supporting financially the parish, one just attending services without obligation, and on occasional on some dates between baptisms and funerals.

The All Saints Parish does Mission work amongst nationalities irrespective of social or financial standing. It needs pecuniary help, but limiting the Parish activity to paying members only, is to betray the laws of charity entrusted to the Catholic Parish. Judging Christ by money leads to treason of the faith. The All Saints Parish shall remain a parish for all seeking Religion and its services.

While expressly welcoming all ethnic groups and stating a willingness to be open for all, the Polish-Americans were aware that "The working man's penny has created the institution of which Religion and City is proud." (Jubilee History, page 24) In another section of the Silver Jubilee book titled "News About The Parish" was found the following paragraph.

While talking of finances it behooves to mention a grading of generosity. What nationality amongst those attending her Church and School is most generous? Here and there are families well situated who have heartedly contributed towards the Parish, but as a group, the Poles have given the biggest share. Some nations do not take any interest in religion, and those coming from such countries have not the least sentiment of duty towards religion. They rather expect the Church to help them. In time though the American spirit will reform them and make them see what obligations befall a citizen.

To the Polish-American members of All Saints, the acceptance of the freedoms offered by the United States brought corresponding obligations. To participate fully in all services and organizations the Polish-American Catholics readily accepted the financial burden of building and maintaining the facilities of the Parish to which they belonged.

All Saints Celebrates 25th Year Jubilee

There had been a fire necessitating reconstruction of the church building so the Jubilee program was postponed until November 1935. The week long festivities emphasized the international qualities of All Saints parish. On Monday evening the Sisters of St. Joseph of the Third Order of Saint Francis (Polish speaking Nuns) directed the school children in a play which included "singing, dancing, tableaus, costumes of many nationalities." (Silver Jubilee Book, page 36) The title of the play was "Flint's Pioneers"; listed below are the nations and the names of the participants. It should be noted that the surnames of the children generally correspond with the nation represented. It appears that the Sisters were drawing from the ethnic cultural traditions of the members of All Saints Parish.

"FLINT'S PIONEERS"

Wanda, a Polish pioneer	Virginia Jasinska
Janek, her husband	Eric Lesinski

NATIONS

French	Ellis Paquette - Gilbertha Mailhot
French Children	Arthur Drinkwine - Lucille Thibeau
Irish, Mrs. Macree	Kathaleen Cavanaugh
Irish Children	Bernadine Anes - Leonard J. Patrick

Italian, Mr. Marino	Peter Mangaracina
Italian, Mrs. Marino	Dorothy Cusenza
Italian Children	Anthony Cusenza - Jeanette Cusenza
German, Mr. Knapps	Ralph Roesner
German, Mrs. Knapps	Rosalia Voight
German Children	Francis Voight - Dolores Kuzma
Bohemian, Mr. Hrabacek	Floyd Tymrok
Bohemian, Mrs. Hrabacek	Ladislava Swierca
Slovene, Mr. Pristliyl	George Kaza
Slovene, Mrs. Pristliyl	Eleanore Niedzielska
Slovene Children	Nicholas Gresock - Rose Wasielewska
Syrian Parents	Louis Maroun - Helen Rashead
Syrian Children	Delores Thomas - Catherine Macksood - William Okal
Turkey	Harold Alle - Frances Alle
Mexican	Jessie Gonzales
Ukrainian	Genevieve Maslanka
Hungarian	Eleanore Kalocy

Spanish	Rose Flores - Mary Flores
Mr. Labraye, Frenchman	Ellisworth DeCaire
Englishman	George Campbell
Italian	Michael Giammonia
Swede	Bernard Kobylik

These CHARACTERS are written in the order of their appearance in the stage production "Flint's Pioneers" commemorating the early years of the establishment of All Saints Parish.

Education for Their Children Was Worth Sacrifice

The Polish people were thinking and planning for the future at the time of their Silver Jubilee, even when there were many past achievements to celebrate. Three Sisters of Saint Joseph began teaching at All Saints in 1915 with an enrollment of 150 children in grades first through seventh. In a section of the Silver Jubilee Book titled, "News About the Parish," their dreams for the future are detailed:

> A church, a rectory, a school old and new, a Sisters' convent and the janitor's quarters. Studies are being made preparatory to the elimination of the entertainment hall on the second floor of the old school building and replacing with a modern gymnasium, adaptable to athletics, shows and dances. The great attendance at doings in the school hall demand an immediate change for safety's sake, for convenience and for size. A hall doubled probably will answer the purpose.

Another reason demanding a change in the hall is the necessity of a high school. The most adequate space would be the second floor where the hall is at present. The demand for a high school is growing with every commencement. Furthermore, the big parishes in Flint like St. Michael, St. Matthew, St. Mary, Mount Morris have each a complete high school. The All Saints Parish, second oldest, after St. Michael, feels the need of an institution of higher learning, and what is important, the parishioners repeatedly have expressed a wish of possessing a high school.

With those changes in view, naturally it becomes necessary to enlarge the Sisters' convent, to make a place for high school teachers and at the same time modernize the 19 year old residence. (All Saints Silver Jubilee Book, pages 20-24)

By 1950 the school building had two additions, a new building for the elementary school and a large modern gymnasium and auditorium combination. The All Saints School football team that year won citywide recognition as Parochial School Champions.

Old All Saints Sacrificed to "Industrial Progress"

The rejoicing and prospering parish received news in 1952 that Buick Motors Company was interested in purchasing the land on which the All Saints Parish complex stood, for a parking lot. Parents transferred their high school children to other schools promising a more stable future education. There was much sadness among the parishioners when the twelve graduating seniors of 1954 received their honors and diplomas in the gymnasium/auditorium, for they were the last. In June of 1957 the elementary school, first through eighth grades, closed its doors with only 135 students left to be transferred to Sacred Heart.

On January 13, 1957 the headlines on Section Two of the newspaper, The Flint Journal read: "All Saints Church Buys New Site." After 47 years of service to the community, the Polish Parish of All Saints was relocating from Industrial Avenue, Maines, and Addison Street, to West Pierson Road. The subtitle of the article read "Sell 14-lot Parcel to Buick." The dreaded rumor was now a reality. The old beautifully constructed structures were all demolished and the ground paved over to provide parking for Buick Motor Company's factory workers.

The new church building on West Pierson Road has a hall in the basement and attached rectory. There was some question of the juridical standing of All Saints Parish when the new church was being built. Rev. Anthony Majchrowski, present pastor, was also pastor then. He said that similar to St. Mary of Czestochowa no written documents could be located to verify its status as a Juridical National Parish but there were verbal reassurances from Bishop Albers and the following directives were given. All parishioners of Old All Saints Parish regardless of nationality and place of residence could join the new parish. All Polish speaking and of Polish descent have the right to join All Saints regardless of place of residence. In addition territorial boundaries were set up to expand the Parish services to the surrounding neighborhoods.

The Polish language has retained a minimal role at All Saints. At one English language Mass on Sundays, the Gospel is read in both Polish and English and a short Homily is preached in both languages. Confessions are heard in both languages. In May and October the Rosary and other Devotional Prayers are said in Polish. There are only about twenty (20) parishioners who speak only Polish and do not understand English. Up to 75% of the parishioners are of Polish descent and desire the retention of Polish customs. An accurate accounting of the number of parishioners was not available but there are 558 envelope numbers. These donation envelopes are distributed to the heads of household and there are many widows and single heads of household living in the area.

The following segment contains descriptions of some of the Polish Catholic traditional expressions of their faith that have been and still are very important to parish life at All Saints.

Polish Traditions Have Always Been a Part of Parish Life at All Saints

Rev. Anthony Majchrowski, the present pastor of All Saints, related in a lengthy conversation that the Polish language has played a lesser role than Polish traditions in Parish life, particularly during the Holy Days of Christmas and Easter Season. Two Polish traditions still perpetuated at All Saints Parish are the "Pasterka," the Shepherd's Mass at midnight Christmas Eve, and "Gorzkie Zale" on the Sundays of lent.

That the Polish language does not have to be understood to be appreciated, is evident at Midnight Mass Christmas Eve. The "Pasterka," Shepherd's Midnight Mass, usually begins with the carolers singing "Koledy." "Koledy" are known today as songs of the Polish Christmastide. They are usually peppy tunes, of good wishes, thanks for the gifts from God and friends, or short folk tales of the events surrounding the birth of Jesus Christ. The following titles of "Koledy" for an article appearing in The Citizen newspaper are familiar and have been sung at All Saints in the past and are beloved today by the many people of different nationalities who crowd the Polish Catholic Churches every year. One priest said at Midnight Mass last Christmas that he wished over-crowding was a problem every Sunday.

The "Koledy" preceding Mass are sung by the whole congregation led by the choir. Lawrence Chominski elaborates:

> The most popular "Koledy" today were composed in the late 18th and 19th centuries, during the period of Partitioned Poland. Set in the identifiable context of impoverished rural Poland, these carols bespeak the national aspirations of the Poles. They are romantically messianic in that the sufferings of Poland are symbolized in the poor, shivering Babe in the manger, born to deliver mankind.

> Among American Polonia the "Koledy" originating from Krakow and, in general, the south-central region of Poland called "Malopolska" are the most widely known and sung. These include "Dzisiaj w Betlejem" (Today in Bethlehem), "Pojdzmy Wszyscy do Stajenki" (Let's All Go to the Stable), and "Sliczna Panienka Jezusa Zrodzila" (A Lovely Maiden Bore Jesus). But the hymnals brought to America from the old country by the immigrants of 80 and 90 years ago also contain beautiful "Koledy" from other regions of Poland, like "Przystapmy do Szopy" (Let's Enter the Stable) from Wielkopolska in the west.

> Difficult, indeed, is the task of ascribing authorship to Polish carols. Some, "Bog Sie Rodzi" (God Is Born) by neoclassical lyricist Franciszek Karpinski (1740-1825), were composed in conscious imitation of the existing tradition and have known authors. Most, however, are anonymous.

This fact further justifies the very special place "Koledy" hold today in the hearts of Poles. As perhaps no other genre of Polish literature or music, the "Koledy" are a commonly and popularly possessed heritage. They were inspired by the most significant event in human history – the birth of the Savior and developed patiently over the centuries. In their own right the "Koledy" continue to inspire artists and to gladden so many hearts at Christmastime. (Chominski, Jan. 8, 1981:10)

Some of the "Koledy" have stanzas that have been translated into English and sung in the Polish melody. This allows for some degree of understanding for those who are not fluent in Polish when these stanzas are interspersed between the traditional ones.

At midnight a procession led by an acolyte carrying a gold crucifix high for all to see, enters the church building. Included in the marchers following him are children who have made their first communion that year, other representatives of age levels, and officers of church organizations. The a young woman dressed as Mary, the Blessed Mother of Jesus, follows carrying a figure of the Christ Child to be placed in the manger which already has statues of Mary and Joseph and animals and some shepherds at a distance from the stable.

Following the young woman are bell-ringers who alternate ringing high and low toned bells, then an incensor, and finally the priest celebrant with a large Host (believed to be the real presence of the body of Christ) held high above his head for all to see. The processional participants vary in number and elaboration of costumes. Each year can be different. One year through standing room only congregation, there were candle bearing marchers intertwined in every aisle. With the lights out it gave a heavenly glow to the faces of all the people whose voices were raised in song in the Polish language which few understood intellectually but all visibly felt in their hearts.

The Mass itself is now in English, the theme is the Old Testament prophesies of the Birth of Christ and New Testament of its fulfillment. The Gospel and Homily are given in both English and Polish.

All Saints makes available to its parishioners and others who seek to maintain the tradition, oplatek. This is a wafer of unleavened bread frequently called "Angel Bread." The traditional use is to distribute these wafers to family and friends after Midnight Mass at a large gathering. After each person has one they each in turn go to another making wishes for the other person, breaking off a small piece from each and eating it before going to the next. Wishes or blessings most common are for peace, health, prosperity, and many time for a "Polish Catholic Marriage Partner."

The time of penance and preparation for Easter in the Catholic Church is called Lent. This Period lasts for forty days, beginning with Ash Wednesday and ending the Saturday before Easter.

The day before Ash Wednesday has been given the name Shrove Tuesday and one does not need to be Polish or speak the language to enjoy the "Paczki," bingo games, and general celebrations of that day, before buckling down to the serious business of penance during Lent. "Paczki" are doughnuts usually filled with prune jelly/jam to symbolize the sweetness in life. In the more Americanized areas, raspberry, or other flavored jellies are offered as alternatives. (Chominski, April 1, 1981:13)

As the American neighborhoods dye their eggs for Easter egg hunts, Polish traditionalists carry on with "pisanki," a method of combining food colors and melted beeswax thus creating an intricate design on either hard boiled eggs or on shells that have been emptied by piercing the shell at each end and blowing out the contents. (Chominski, April 1, 1981:13)

"Swiecone" – the blessing of selected foods on Holy Saturday for consumption on Easter morning enjoys immense popularity. Once confined to Polish and other Slavic churches, the custom has gained acceptance in purely territorial Catholic parishes. But again, to take a food basket sprigged with pussy willows to church for a prayer and sprinkle of holy water does not require fluency in an ancestral tongue. (Chominski, April 1, 1981:13)

The following information about

"Food Blessing/Swieconka" was added

December 20, 2007.

Swieconka is one of the most enduring and beloved Polish traditions.

On the Saturday before Easter, people take to churches decorated baskets containing a sampling of traditional food to be blessed. Each food has a symbolic meaning, for example:

Eggs (Hard boiled or "Pisanki") symbolize life and Christ's resurrection,

Bread – symbolic of Jesus, the Bread of Life,

Butter Lamb – represents Christ, the Lamb of God,

Salt – represents purification,

Horseradish – symbolic of the bitter sacrifice of Christ,

Ham or sausage or both – symbolic of great joy and abundance.

The food blessed in church remains untouched until Easter Sunday morning breakfast.

"Gorzkie Zale" or Bitter Sorrows is a series of devotional prayers and lamentations, including one dialogue between a woman singing the part of Mary, the Blessed Mother of Jesus, and the penitent congregation who represent all people who ever lived.

Lawrence Chominski offered to his readers this "Waliklo" translation:

-- AH, I am a sorrowing Mother, unbearable pain tortures me. A sword pierced my heart.

    -- Why, beloved Mother, is your heart so troubled? Why are you fainting?

-- Why ask me this? I cannot speak when so weakened by tears. My heart drowns in blood.

    -- Tell me, my Lady, why is your face so pale? Why the bitter tears?

-- I see my beloved in Gethsemane, bathed in streams of bloody sweat.

    -- O Mother, fountainhead of love, may I feel your pangs of sorrow; allow me to weep with you! (Chominski, April 16, 1981:15)

"Gorzkie Zale" mysteriously draws non-Polish speaking observers year after year. The sorrowful melodies fulfill some need, for this traditional service is still held in Polish every year at All Saints Church at popular request.

Theory Relationships

All Saints is in a special position. Although it officially is a Juridical Nation Parish, when it was relocated, it was also given territorial boundaries. Parishioners of Polish descent live within over twenty other territorial parish boundaries. All Saints remains a bilingual, bicultural Polish parish, but with more of an international membership. Traditions hold more importance than the Polish language although from its founding to the present day, there has been a Polish speaking resident pastor. Its unique position of dual status with territorial boundaries and language protection may move All Saints in another direction. It may become totally Americanized or with a resurgence of ethnicity may experience a revival of the Polish-Catholic parish life, that it had at one time shared with the surrounding community.

As the neighborhood membership increases, the percentage of Polish-Americans still maintaining membership at All Saints steadily decreases. Young families find it difficult to travel many miles so instead they join nearer territorial parishes. All Saints has kept a steady course throughout its history, whether it will continue to do so depends on the extent of the Polish-American ethnic demands.

Industrial progress affected the community surrounding All Saints. The Americanization forces came basically from the expansion of General Motors, with residential areas being wiped away to make room for larger factories. The first site of All Saints Parish is now replaced by a parking lot. Instead of people moving away, the church building and the center of parish life was relocated. Not all parishioners, even if they so desired, were able to live near the new church. Many of the elderly still seek rides to All Saints but All Saints needs young life if it is to remain vital and strong. These younger parishioners come from varied hereditary backgrounds. All speak English, all enjoy the Polish traditions, particularly around the holiday seasons of Christmas and Easter, but to them the Polish American Catholic traditions are not an integral part of their parish life.

All Saints does not have a renewal program in Service of Tradition as does St. Albertus. All Saints did not have to fight to retain its Polishness as did St. Mary of Czestochowa's parishioners. One danger to the retention of Polish traditions at all Saints that could develop would be complacency. There presently are few overt economic or social pressures to change. There is a continuity and stability in the parish that is unusual for an urban parish but how long it will remain Polish if the pastor dies or many of the older Polish-Americans is questionable. The newer non-Polish parishioners' support keeps the financial balance at All Saints, so as a territorial parish there is little question of its survival.

The "Triple Melting Pot" theory, that an "American Catholic" would emerge from exposure to many cultural differences, did not materialize. Of the three parishes studied All Saints could be expected to exemplify this theory with the international composition of its membership. How can one explain that through industrialization, social/economic mobility, American born children to the fifth generation, and exposure to many varied beautiful experiences with culturally different ethnic groups, All Saints manages to preserve its Polish-American Catholic character.

6. Conclusions and Analyses

The official motto on the seal of the United States was changed from "E Pluribus Unum" to "In God We Trust" in 1956. Could this have been recognition of the near impossibility of forming, "out of many, one" American nationality? This change coincided with the resurgence of ethnicity.

During a symposium at the Smithsonian Institute, the book, The Cultural Drama evolved.

The topic, "Cultural Styles and Social Identities: Interpretations of Protest and Change" (Dillon, 1974:26), literally came to life as the audience protested the lack of youth, women, and ethnic representations in the program. The Smithsonian Institute selected cultural pluralism as an indispensable feature of the American way of life. The members called for "Down with homogenization." (Dillon, 1974:34) But, up with what? Suggestions of "constructive marginality" and "diversity by design" were two of the choices. The Juridical National Parish within the Roman Catholic Church in the United States fits both perspectives. The National parish is marginal, as the territorial parish is the more common accepted form of external organization. The Polish-American liturgies, services, and traditions are definitely diverse by design. The symposium raised some basic questions relating to cultural change.

> (1) What are the internal and external factors that generate shifts in rates and types of culture change? (2) What are the processes by which culture change takes place? (3) What models and methods are now available for the study of culture and change? And (4) How is the concept of culture change related to the closely associated phenomena of diffusion, innovation, evolution, acculturation, and nativism? (Dillon, 1974:29)

Some answers to these questions were discovered in this research. In the first proposed question, "What are the internal and external factors that generate shifts in rates and types of culture change?" a problem arises with definitions of internal and external. If internal is to be defined within the context of the Catholic Church in the United States, where does the Pope fit in as head of the entire Roman Catholic Church. His role definitely affected the parishes in the United States. Pope Leo XIII feared that Americanizing forces were a disguise for protestant values infiltration. Then the removal of mission status in 1908 gave more authority to American bishops. The first action gave a push to the hierarchy toward cultural pluralism, the second swung sentiments back toward Americanization.

External factors when defined as outside of the United States would include wars, famines, and in Poland the partitioning into three sectors in 1772. Corresponding internal elements would involve immigrant concentration in certain areas, immigration quotas limiting the percentage of Poles represented in the general population, and artificial infighting within Polish communities. One problem of cultural identification came with the registering of Polish immigrants. In county census data, Prussian Poles, Russian Poles, Austrian Poles, and German Poles were listed. Less frequently, only the word Polish was listed. In more than ten percent of the listings, a Polish sounding last name had Germany or Russia registered under "previous residence" and in later years under "place of birth." This could be expected for in 1870, when the German empire was formed Poles were forced to learn German and deny their heritage. The Roman Catholic Church remained the only expression of their Polishness.

When external is taken to mean outside the single parish life, and internal means the leadership, organization, and the congregation, other factors emerge to generate cultural changes. It has generally been accepted that the Catholic Church in the United States served as a social institution to Americanize immigrants. Again definitions of what is American led to different interpretations.

The cultural pluralist definition would hold American to be synonymous with diversity. The Assimilationist would mean the Anglo-Saxon tradition, but with the addition of Irish in the Catholic Church.

Just as the presiding Popes influenced the direction of cultural changes, the Bishops and Pastors affected the character of each of these Parishes. The perspective of the Bishop establishes the priorities in his diocese. Bishop Borgess of Detroit wanted St. Albertus to be financially sound and had little ethnic sympathies, but stressed the unity among Catholics in rhetoric and processions, putting him in the Americanization quarters. Archbishop Dearden definitely held cultural pluralistic values and fostered ethnicity at St. Albertus.

Bishop Foley of Detroit, while advocating the "Melting Pot" theory for Catholics nevertheless, established both St. Mary of Czestochowa and All Saints Juridical National Parishes. Bishop Reh of Saginaw spoke, advocating a "melting pot" for the parishes under his jurisdiction, but in actions did not appear to have a place in his scheme for "Polishness" to contribute to the whole new American Catholic. His view of "The American Catholic Parish" was peculiarly his own interpretation of the recommendations of the Second Vatican Council. From the initiatives of Bishop Untener, who succeeded Bishop Reh, it appears he has some understanding of ethnic values.

Bishop Joseph Albers of the Lansing Diocese although not Polish, respected the rights of All Saints as a Juridical National Parish when its physical transfer was mandated by the industrial encroachment of General Motors. The two most recent Bishops in Lansing, Bishop Alexander Zaleski, and Bishop Kenneth Povish, both of Polish ancestry allowed All Saints the privileges of maintaining its ethnic character combined with territorial standing. Neither the new American members, nor the Polish-American parishioners are treated as second class individuals.

Pastors in interaction with the congregation have also affected the rate of culture change and direction of these changes. The stormy history of St. Albertus reveals the strong influence pastors can have on the parishioners as well as the public and the press. The pastor's sensitivity to ethnic values can sway the sentiments of the people, but to the dismay of some and the success of others, certain areas seem impervious to assimilation.

The low profile of the pastors at St. Mary of Czestochowa indicates that their feelings or fear of reprisal kept them from taking a stand on either side of the ethnicity question. The conflict primarily was between Bishop Reh and the parishioners. This may be a sign of the times where in a democracy the people did not accept the dictates of authority without question and instead found leadership in a committee rather than a pastor.

Reverend Anthony Majchrowski, an eloquent preacher in both Polish and English serves all members of All Saints equally. His Polish ancestry and American training fit him beautifully into a pattern of "diversity by design." Having grown up in the international climate of Old All Saints, his rapport with his parishioners reflects mutual respect. The style of cultural pluralism in evidence at All Saints could possibly serve as a sociological model for other American Institutions.

Other external factors affecting the rate and types of culture change in these three parishes were industrialization and the social/economic mobility of parishioners. The most volatile and mobile community is Detroit. Within a small radius there existed only five years ago, three Polish parishes. In a socially and economically mobile climate, the first generation American born of Polish descent tried to assimilate and thus obtain a piece of the "good life." Some moved to the suburbs and changed their names, but came back to

St. Albertus for baptisms, marriages, and funerals. City planning or lack of it allowed the construction of factories and freeways to virtually destroy the viable community life of the remaining Polish-Americans, including the actual destruction of one church and the adjacent buildings. Ethnic awareness or resurgence may have come too late to return St. Albertus Parish to its former magnificent stature and numbers, for there simply is no room to house new and growing families.

Industrialization has had little affect on the character of St. Mary of Czestochowa Parish. The farms in the area are more productive. Equipment and houses are modern, making life easier for the residents. Among the first generation Polish-Americans there was no need to change their names to prosper or be accepted, for the family farms kept two or three generations well fed. They enjoyed the security of a sheltered Polish community. Even the territorial parish, St. Edward has fifty percent Polish-American parishioners. St. Mary of Czestochowa serves as a home base for the Polish-Americans that seek employment in the cities in professions that cannot be supported in Dwight Township. For these descendants St. Mary of Czestochowa provides the connection with their heritage.

Similar to Detroit, industrialization dramatically affected the course of All Saints history. As the factories encroached on the residential areas, houses were purchased for expansion, reducing available members. The quality of life was lowered by higher levels of air and noise pollution, making it less desirable community. Emotions were torn in many directions with faithful members holding out until General Motor forced them out of their homes and businesses by building fences around their property or big pipes just outside their windows. With the cooperation of the Bishops, All Saints was able to rise again, but not to former heights. They have no school. Their meeting rooms are in the basement of the church.

No auditorium exists for Polish wedding receptions, athletic competitions, or the traditional dramatic presentations with their international flavor. All Saints has ceased to be the focal point of community life, but does provide a link with the past in name, language, religious services, and traditions.

In answer to the second question proposed by the symposium, it can be stated that the processes by which culture change take place are as complex as society and family life. An attempt has been made in this paper to simply identify the forces and the role each factor has played in the retention of the ethnic character of the three Polish Parishes.

The third question raised at the Smithsonian Institute, "What models and methods are now available for the study of culture and changes?" was partially answered with the call for a new model. At the Symposium it was agreed that the available models of assimilation, the melting pot, and cultural pluralism fall short of describing the actualities of American life. These models more readily serve the purpose of studying what the proponents think American life should be.

Study methods are more sophisticated for both collection of data, cross-referencing, and analyzing. Computers facilitate these methods, as well as storing and distributing information. This enables sociologists to concentrate on one facet while drawing on current research. Communication through world-wide television coverage allows observations and comparisons of political, cultural, and social arenas previously unexplored.

The last question "How is the concept of culture change related to the closely associated phenomena of diffusion, innovation, evolution, acculturation, and nativism?" can be investigated within the context of the role played by the Juridical National Parish in the evolution of the American Catholic Church. The Catholic Church had missions on the North American continent long before the United States and its government were established, yet it was not considered a native institution, because of the affiliation with Rome and the percentage of Catholics in the population was negligible. Only with the influx of south and east European immigrants did Catholics begin to pose a numerical threat to Anglo-Saxon domination and subsequently the Catholic Church was labeled the inferior immigrant church of the laboring classes. This precipitated the Americanization movement by American Bishops and priests. These forces in turn offended ethnic groups' sensitivities of first the Germans, then the Poles. In the midst of this turmoil the Juridical National Parish evolved as a compromise.

The three Polish-American Catholic Parishes, All Saints in particular, represent in microcosm the essence of American culture as proposed by the Smithsonian Institute Symposium. The threads of Polish-Catholic institutions, traditions, and values are intricately interwoven with American urban, rural, industrial, democratic, equalitarian conditions to create a tapestry reflecting diversity by design.

Diversity exists within the Roman Catholic Parishes in the United State and even within the narrow context of Polish Language Juridical National Parishes. The degrees of assimilation and the present roles of each individual parish has been affected by geographical locations, hierarchical decisions, individual personalities and their cultural preferences among both the clergy and the laity.

Social and economic forces combined with the persistence of cultural pluralism, shape the congregation and roles of these three parishes today.

This research revealed that the Polish Juridical National Parishes did not disappear as expected, but were transmuted by succeeding generations to fulfill their ethnic needs. From this study, it can be concluded that the Polish-American Catholic Parishes will continue, in some form, to flourish in Michigan in the United States of America.

7. REFERENCES

Abbott, Walter M., Ed.1966,   The Documents of Vatican II
New York: Guild Press, American Press, Association Press

Andres, Theodore 1953,   The Polish National Catholic Church in
America and Poland, London: S.P.C.K.

Biever, Bruce Francis 1976,   Religion, Culture, and Values,
New York: Arno Press

Boucher, Arline and Tehan, John 1962, Prince of Democracy:
James Cardinal Gibbons, Garden City, New York: Hanover House

Bouscaren, T. Lincoln, Second Edition, Canon Law, Milwaukee:
The Bruce Publishing Company

Canfield, Francis X., 1962 Development of the Catholic Church in
the Great Lakes Region, Detroit, Michigan: Burton Historical
Collection

Cogley, John, 1973, Catholic America, New York: The Dial Press

Dillon, Wilton S., Ed., 1974, The Cultural Drama,   Washington:
Smithsonian Institution Press

Dohen, Dorothy, 1967, Nationalism and American Catholicism
New York: Sheed and Ward

Dolan, Jay P., 1975,   The Immigrant Church, New York's Irish and
German Catholics, 1815-1865,   Baltimore and London:
The John Hopkins University Press

Egan, Patrick K., 1968,   The Influence of the Irish on the Catholic
Church in America in the Nineteenth Century Dublin: National
University of Ireland

Eitzen, Stanley D., 1978,   In Conflict and Order, Boston, London:
Allyn and Bacon, Inc.

Ellis, John Trach, 1956,   Documents of American Catholic History
Milwaukee: The Bruce Publishing Co.

Fox, Paul, 1922,   The Poles in America, New York:
George H. Doran Company, Reprint Edition, Arno Press, Inc., 1970

Fry, C. Luther, 1922,The New and the Old Immigrant on the Land,
New York: George H. Doran Company

Glazer, Nathan, and Moynihan, Daniel P., 1963,
Beyond the Melting Pot, Cambridge, Massachusetts:
    The Massachusetts Institute of Technology Press

Gleason, Philip, Ed., 1970,   Catholicism in America, New York:
Harper and Row Publishers, Inc.

Gordon, Milton M., 1964,   Assimilation in American Life
New York, Oxford University Press, Inc., Reprint Edition, 1974

Greeley, Andrew M., 1977,   The American Catholic,
New York: Basic Books, Inc., Publishers

Greeley, Andrew M., 1971,   Come Blow Your Mind with Me,
Garden City, New York: Doubleday and Company, Inc.

Greene, Victor, 1975,   For God and Country,   Madison,
Wisconsin: The State Historical Society of Wisconsin

Guilday, Peter, 1923, The National Pastorale of the American
Hierarchy (1792-1919),   Washington, D. C.: National Catholic
Welfare Council

Hayes, Frederic H., 1965, Michigan Catholicism in the Era of the
Civil War,   Lansing, Michigan: Michigan War Centennial
Observance Commission

Haiman, Miescislaus, 1975, Polish Past in America, Chicago: Polish Museum of America

Herberg, Will, 1955, Protestant-Catholic-Jew, Garden City, New York: Doubleday and Company, Inc., Reprint Edition, 1960

Holi, Melvin G. and Jones, Peter d'A, 1977, The Ethnic Frontier, Michigan: William B. Ferdmans Publishing Co.

Kuniczak, W. S., 1978, My Name Is Milton, Garden City, New York: Doubleday and Co., Inc.

Lally, Francis J., 1962, The Catholic Church in a Changing America, Boston, Toronto: Little Brown and Company

Leckie, Robert, 1970, American and Catholic, New York: Doubleday and Company, Inc.

Lopata, Helena Ananiecki, 1976, Polish Americans, Status Competition in an Ethnic Community, New Jersey: Prentice Hall, Inc.

McAvoy, Thomas T., 1970, A History of the Catholic Church in the United States, Notre Dame, Indiana: University of Notre Dame Press

McAvoy, Thomas T.; Nye, Russel B.; Wiley, Jay W.; McGree, Gale W.; Murphy, Donald R.: Flanagan, John T.: Frederick, John T., 1961, Illinois & Indiana: University of Notre Dame Press

Miller, Randall M. and Marzik, Thomas D., 1977, Immigrants and Religion in Urban America, Philadelphia: Temple University Press

Milostan, Harry, ed.,1977, Parisville Poles, First Polish Settlers in U.S.A., Mt. Clemens, Michigan: Masspac Publishing Company

Natsolim, 1977, Enduring Poles, Mt. Clemens, Michigan: Masspac Publishing Company

Niebuhr, Reinhold, 1952, The Irony of American History, New York: Charles Scribner's Sons

Niebuhr, Reinhold, 1963, A Nation So Conceived, New York: Charles Scribner's Sons

Novak, Michael, 1972,   The Rise of the Unmeltable Ethnics, New York: The MacMillan Company

Nuesse, C. J. and Harte, Thomas, 1950, The Sociology of the Parish, Milwaukee: The Bruce Publishing Company

Orton, Lawrence D., 1981, Polish Detroit and the Kolasinski Affair, Detroit: Wayne State University Press

Putz, Louis J., 1956, The Catholic Church, U.S.A.,   Chicago: Fides Publishers Association

Ryan, Joseph A., 1973, White Ethnics: Life in Working-Class America, New Jersey: Prentice-Hall, Inc.

Stanczyk, Benjamin C.; Konstantynowicz, Eugene; Kathnaw, Anthony: Wioszczewski, Stefan L.; Brominski, Eugene; Wojsowski, Anthony, 1955,   Editorial Committee, Poles in Michigan, Detroit, Michigan: The Poles in Michigan, Associated

Sugrue, Francis, 1961, Popes in the Modern World, New York: Thomas Y. Crowell Company

Swastek, Joseph, 1973,   Detroit's Oldest Polish Parish, St. Albertus 1872-1973 Centennial, Detroit, Michigan

Vollmar, Edward R.,1956, The Catholic Church in America, New Jersey: The Scarecrow Press

Wood, Arthur Evans, 1955,   Hamtramck Then and Now, New York: Bookman Associates

Wrobel, Paul, 1979, Our Way, Notre Dame, Indiana: University of Notre Dame Press

Wytrwal, Joseph A., 1969, Poles in America History and Tradition, Detroit, Michigan: Endurance Press

Zinn, Maxine Baca, 1980, "Employment and Education of Mexican American Women: The Interplay of Modernity and Ethnicity in Eight Families," Harvard Educational Review, Vol. 50, No. 1.

NEWSPAPER ARTICLES

Chominski, Lawrence, 1980,   The Citizen, October 9

Chominski, Lawrence, 1981,   The Citizen, January 8

Chominski, Lawrence, 1981,   The Citizen, April 9

Mroczek, Patricia, 1980,   The Huron Daily Tribune, August 25

Trbovich, Marco, 1973,   Detroit Free Press, March 25

Flint Journal, The, 1957,   Reporter not indicated, January 13

Huron Daily Tribune, 1980,   Reporter not indicated, November 13

Pol/Am (Polish/American) Journal, 1980,   Reporter not indicated (Article in scrapbook of Ralph Majeski)

INTERVIEWS

Ferrara, Jenny, 1981, By telephone, June 18

Majchrowski, Anthony, 1981,   By telephone, April 28

Majchrowski, Anthony, 1981,   By telephone, June 18

Majchrowski, Anthony, 1981,   At All Saints Rectory, July 26

Majeski, Ralph, 1980,   At his home, September 28

Matlenga, Joseph, 1980,   By telephone, November 10

www.ingramcontent.com/pod-product-compliance
Lightning Source LLC
Chambersburg PA
CBHW072325290526
45794CB00002B/751